VIOLENT DUALITY

a study of
Margaret Atwood

Two voices
took turns using my eyes:
                              ("The Double Voice," *JSM*)

        to take
That risk, to offer life and remain

alive, open yourself like this and become whole
                              ("Book of Ancestors," *YAH*)

VIOLENT DUALITY

a study of Margaret Atwood

by
Sherrill Grace

EDITED BY KEN NORRIS

Véhicule Press

For two Elizabeths:
Mother and Daughter

Excerpts from *Dancing Girls* by Margaret Atwood reprinted by permission of the Canadian Publishers, McClelland & Stewart Limited, Toronto.

"We Don't Like Reminders" from *Procedures for Underground* by Margaret Atwood reprinted by permission of Oxford University Press.

Quotes from *Two-Headed Poems* © Margaret Atwood 1978, reprinted by permission of the publisher Oxford University Press, Canada.

Permission for general quotation from her works granted by Margaret Atwood.

Canadian Cataloguing in Publication Data
Grace, Sherrill, 1944.
    Violent duality
Includes index.
Bibliography: p.
ISBN: 0-919890-22-9 bd. ISBN: 0-919890-23-7 pa.
1. Atwood, Margaret, 1939-   —Criticism and interpretation. I. Title.
PS8501.T86Z64 C813'.54 C80-090029-4
PR9199.3.A88Z64

Published with the assistance of the Canada Council.

Véhicule Press, P.O.B. 125, Station "La Cité", Montreal, Canada H2X 3M0

Dépôt légal, Bibliothèque nationale du Québec, National Library of Canada, 1er trimestre, 1980.
Printed in Canada.

Table of Contents

Abbreviations

Margaret Atwood: Biography

1939, November	— born in Ottawa, Canada
1939-1945	— Ottawa; northern Quebec in spring, summer and fall
1945	— Sault Ste. Marie
1946-1961	— Toronto; trips to northern Ontario and Quebec in spring, summer and fall
1961	— B.A., Victoria College, University of Toronto — E. J. Pratt Medal, for *Double Persephone*
1961-1963	— Boston, Massachusetts.
1962	— M.A., Radcliffe College, Harvard University
1963-1965	— Toronto, job in market research; wrote first novel, unpublished
1964-1965	— Vancouver, teaching composition and literature at the University of British Columbia; writing *The Edible Woman*
1965	— President's Medal, University of Western Ontario
1965-1967	— Boston, Massachusetts
1966	— Governor General's Award for *The Circle Game*
1967	— Centennial Commission Poetry Competition, First, for *The Animals in that Country*
1967-1968	— Montreal, teaching Victorian and American literature at Sir George Williams University
1968-1970	— Edmonton, writing *Procedures for Underground* and *Power Politics*
1969	— Union Poetry Prize, *Poetry* (Chicago)
1969-1970	— teaching Creative Writing at the University of Alberta
1970-1971	— London, England; France; Italy — writing *Surfacing*
1971-1972	— Toronto, teaching literature and creative writing at York University

1971-1973	— Toronto, working with House of Anansi Press
1972-1973	— Toronto, Writer-in-Residence at the University of Toronto
1973	— D. Litt., Trent University
1973	— moves to Alliston, Ontario where she now lives with Graeme Gibson
1974	— LL.D., Queen's University
	— The Bess Hopkins Prize, *Poetry* (Chicago), for the animal poems in *You Are Happy*
1976, May	— daughter, Jess, is born
1977	— The City of Toronto Book Award, for *Lady Oracle*
	— The Canadian Bookseller's Association Award, for *Lady Oracle*
	— writing *Two-Headed Poems*
1978-1979	— writing *Life Before Man*
	— winter in Scotland

Preface

" A Piece of art," Margaret Atwood writes in *Survival*, " as well as being a creation to be enjoyed, can also be ... a mirror.... If a country or a culture lacks such mirrors it has no way of knowing what it looks like; it must travel blind." Criticism can also be a mirror, one that helps us see the artist, and the art. The relationship between criticism and art is much like that between art and national culture; both trace or reflect patterns which help us to 'see.' This is what I hope the present study will achieve: read *in conjunction with* the poems and fiction the present book should be a mirror that reflects, with some clarity and accuracy, Margaret Atwood's work.

To achieve clarity, however, is neither easy nor passive, and certain critical assumptions and choices have determined the size and style of this mirror. This book is not a study of the writer. At some future date a critical biographer will undoubtedly face that task. For the present, it is more important to forget the personality of the biographical Margaret Atwood in order to concentrate on her work. I have not attempted, either, to discuss Atwood from a specific critical perspective, structuralist, feminist, or other. This book is intended, however, as an interpretive guide to form and theme in Atwood's work for readers and students. I have tried to keep the scholarly apparatus unobtrusive, and chapter notes appear together at the end of the book. Because Atwood is so prolific a writer, I have devoted my attention to what we can begin to call the central Atwood canon, six books of poetry (her seventh is in press as I write), three novels (she is currently writing a fourth), one collection of short stories and one critical book. She has also written numerous uncollected poems, reviews and critical articles (of which House of Anansi is preparing a collection), a children's book, *Up in the Tree*, a volume of history, and plays. She has worked on filmscripts and contributes a regular comic strip, "Canadian Kultur Komics," to *This Magazine* under the pen-name Bart Gerrard.

Keeping up with, let alone discussing, such a versatile and evolving writer presents a formidable challenge. Any discussion of the poetry, stories or novels must necessarily be explorative; it will be some time yet before a so-called 'definitive' Atwood study can be initiated. Nevertheless, my interpretation has been shaped by the sense of pervasive duality in her art. In chapter I, I treat *Survival* as the mirror, not only of her subjects, but also of her view of art, of the creative process, and of perception, as well as of duality. The image in the mirror of *Survival* comprises not so much "Canadian literature" as the assumptions, methods and concerns of its author. In chapters II to IV, I discuss the poetry from the early poems, including *Double Persephone*, to *You Are Happy*; the fiction is examined chronologically in chapters V to VII. Chapter VIII provides some evaluation and summary as well as brief comments upon *Two-Headed-Poems* of which I was fortunate to see an unedited typescript before completing this study.

My thanks go to the University of British Columbia for the grant that assisted the preparation of the typescript, to my typist Lynda Solberg, and to colleagues who discussed Atwood's work with me. Thanks also to Ken Norris, my editor, who first suggested an Atwood study and has been encouraging throughout, to Alan Horne for prompt bibliographical help, to Rachel Grover of the Thomas Fisher Rare Book Library at the University of Toronto who arranged for me to see manuscript material, and to Oxford University Press for a copy of the *Two-Headed Poems* typescript. To my husband who has read and commented upon the manuscript, my thanks as always. I am especially grateful to Margaret Atwood who has been helpful and generous from start to finish.

S.E.G.
July, 1978

Chapter I

The Image in the Mirror

To live in prison is to live without mirrors.
To live without mirrors is to live without the self.
"Marrying the Hangman" *(THP)*

In the introductory pages of *Survival*, Atwood points out that her study does more than map the "key patterns" of our literature which, in turn, reflect "a national habit of mind."[1] *Survival* is "a cross between a personal statement... and a political manifesto" (p. 13). As a cultural map, or even as a map of Canadian literature, *Survival* is only a rough guide to a hitherto little-known country. Although she makes some interesting discoveries, the study is hampered by its historical limits; it discusses works written chiefly between the 1930's and the end of the sixties, thus neglecting the nineteenth and early twentieth centuries. The resulting emphasis on modern works creates the impression that an obsession with survival and the creation of victims, common in Canadian realist fiction and modern poetry, is synonymous with Canadian literature. Whether or not the struggle for survival is of special significance to Canadians, it is definitely a central problem for modern Western man, and varyingly pessimistic treatments of the idea characterize much modern philosophy and art.

As personal statement and political manifesto, however, *Survival* is more informative. Clearly, Atwood deplores the colonialism which until recently crippled the arts in Canada. She pleads that we come to know ourselves in order to appreciate what we already have. But *Survival* reflects the ideas of its author in other, more subtle ways. Once again, in the introductory pages, Atwood outlines her theory of literature:

A piece of art, as well as being a creation to be enjoyed, can also be... a mirror. The reader looks at the mirror and sees not the writer but himself; and behind his own image in the foreground, a reflection of the world he lives in. (*S*, p. 15)

1

Literature, then, is mimetic. It provides us with a picture of man and his world. This picture, as the concept of mimesis itself, should not be simplistically interpreted as a copy or reproduction of objective reality because the work of art shapes its mirror world in significant patterns that allow us to see ourselves in new ways. The distinction to be made here is not between art and reality, but between a mimetic theory of art and an expressive one. In *Survival* and elsewhere Atwood makes it clear that she does not think of her art as expressive of an inner world, of the self. She has remarked that if she wanted to express herself she would not write poems, but "go out in the back field and scream."[2]

Atwood's theory of art is closely linked to her views on the nature of the self and human perception. Both of these are discussed at some length in the following chapters of this book as they are central to her work. Because she has too often been accused of writing solipsistically, of creating an obsessively private poetic world in which reality is merely an extension of the self, a few general remarks on these views are in order at this point. Atwood conceives of the self not as an individual ego, defining itself against its surroundings, but as a place or entity co-extensive with its environment. Practically, this view is difficult to maintain; if you stub your toe, you find that the self has boundaries which separate it from out there. Physiologically and metaphorically, however, the idea is accurate and powerful: we are fluid and need not be locked into ourselves. Holding such a view, it is unlikely that expressive art would be Atwood's medium. While she is emphatically anti-solipsistic, she is quick to point out that the world we perceive is, in some measure, a world we create. The idea pervades *Survival*, reaching its clearest statement in the final chapter "Jail-Breaks and Re-creations." The chapter title is drawn from Margaret Avison's poem "Snow" and Atwood's interpretation of Avison's lines explains her attitude towards perception: "What these three lines suggest is that in none of our acts — even the act of looking — are we passive" (p. 246). If we accept this responsibility, we will be able to change our old ways of seeing and re-create a world we "have helped to shape."

Atwood's view of perception is not original, but when it is coupled with her view of the self and her basically mimetic theory of art, an interesting problem arises. If there is an objective world out there but, at the same time, we help to shape that world through our perception of it, then our world and our articulations of it, our poems and novels, will be both expressive and mimetic, expressions

2

of ourselves as well as reflections of objective reality. Philosophically, the dilemma is an ancient one, and in Atwood's poetry and fiction it generates a dynamic tension. The speaker in her poems, or the protagonist in her novels, swings back and forth between a solipsistic extreme, withdrawal into the self, and an absorption or submergence in objective reality, the false perceptions of others or the natural world. Both extremes are destructive as is the process of swinging back and forth which is another form of circle game. Freedom, Atwood implies, does not come from denying or transcending the subject/object duality of life; it is not duality but polarity that is destructive. Freedom comes from accepting the duality or, to use the more precise scientific term, duplicity which we share with all living things as Atwood, daughter of a biologist, well knows. From *Double Persephone* through to *Two-Headed Poems*, Atwood explores the concept of duplicity thematically and formally, always with an ironic eye to its common meaning of deceit. Duplicity, then, is a touchstone in her art, describing the dynamic tension of her creative process and illuminating the personal statement in *Survival*.

Although it is not necessary to discuss *Survival* in great detail, I would like to draw attention to elements of the book that are of particular relevance to Atwood's own poetry and fiction. Many of the examples she discusses in order to make a given point are drawn from other poets who have influenced her or with whom she shares a marked affinity — D.C. and F.R. Scott, James Reaney, Margaret Avison, Jay Macpherson and Dennis Lee, for example. To trace these influences and affinities is not my task — to know Atwood's work for itself precedes any attempt at comparisons — but I have ventured here and there, especially in chapter VIII, to speculate upon her tradition. Of more immediate importance are the thematic patterns which she analyses in *Survival*.

The most infamous of these is, of course, the victim theory with its concept of struggle for survival. Victimization is a common Atwood theme treated with far more subtlety than is often allowed. To be sure, in *Surfacing*, the protagonist states baldly that she must choose not to be a victim, but there are a bewildering number of ways to be a victim, as poems like "The Circle Game" (*CG*), "They Eat Out (*PP*), and "Circe/Mud Poems" (*YAH*), reveal. More important, the struggle not to be victimized becomes a moral imperative; passive acquiescence does not absolve guilt or remove responsibility. In *Lady Oracle*, a delightful parody of much in *Survival*, Joan Foster enacts an exaggerated escape/survival pattern.

But the joke is partial, for Atwood is re-working, in comic form, a serious dilemma — the over-lapping of a "cozy safe domestic" world with "the world of dangers" — which she finds characteristic of Canadian children's fiction in *Survival*:

> this was a world of frozen corpses, dead gophers, snow, dead children, and the ever-present feeling of menace, not from an enemy set over against you but from everything surrounding you. (*S*, p. 30)

In realistic fiction or tragedy, the intrusion of danger into a domestic world leads to catastrophe; in comedy or Gothic romance it leads to confusions or a sequence of threat and escape.

The attitude toward nature that Atwood describes in *Survival* is emphatically Canadian — the double think which D.C. Scott describes as "the beauty of terror the beauty of peace" in "At Gull Lake: August, 1810." As an example of the split in Canadian sensibilities, this love/hate attitude becomes a controlling metaphor in *The Journals of Susanna Moodie* and in the title sequence from *Two-Headed Poems*. Once again, however, it is not duality so much as our determination to polarize our experience that is destructive. A common metaphor for this polarization involves straight line confronting curved space. The pioneer goes progressively insane in his futile effort to impose linear order upon this land. He is, however, slightly mad to begin with, as the title — "Progressive Insanities of a Pioneer" (*AC*) — implies, because he has imposed the rigid order of rationality upon the curved spaces of his mind. This adversary relationship of victor/victim is not inescapable, however. In her description of what nature would look like from "Victim Position Four," Atwood suggests that,

> man himself is seen as part of the process; he does not define himself as "good" or "weak" as against a hostile Nature, or as "bad" or "aggressive" as against a passive, powerless Nature.... Since he does not see life as something that can only be maintained inside a fortress and at the expense of shutting out Nature and sex, he is free to move *within* space rather than in a self-created tank *against* it. (*S*, p. 63)

Nowhere in the poetry or fiction does Atwood offer answers to this problem of polarity. Where she comes closest to affirmation, as in "A Place: Fragments" (*CG*), or "Book of Ancestors" (*YAH*), or the final pages of *Surfacing*, it is in terms of accepting duality *within* the *process* of living.

Another concept in *Survival* that particularly reflects the themes of Atwood's work is that of the Triple Goddess. Women in Canadian literature, she contends, appear as Hecate figures, chilly nasty old women: "Diana-Maidens often die young. There is a notable absence of Venuses. And there is a bumper crop of sinister Hecate-Crones" (p. 199). Atwood offers two explanations for the prevalance of Canadian Hecates: in a land of snow and blackflies, the choice of woman/nature images is limited, and the conservative nature of our society causes us to regard sexual love with suspicion; Hecates, or even Dianas, are safer. Associated with these incomplete symbolic portrayals of woman are the "Great Canadian Baby" fallacy and the "Rapunzel Syndrome." Because the usual role of Venus — sexual love and procreation — is largely absent, babies appear in our novels without being integral to the story; they are born to Dianas or Hecates and tend to be either unconvincing as symbols of new life or threatening. The pattern of the "Rapunzel Syndrome" as it appears in Canadian literature denies escape. Rescuers are useless because *"Rapunzel and the tower are the same"* (p. 209):

> These heroines have internalized the values of their culture to such an extent that they have become their own prisons. The *real* struggle... is the struggle of the Diana, capable of freedom, and of the "good" Venus, capable of love both maternal and sexual, to find a way out of the rigid Hecate stereotype in which she finds herself shut like a moth in a chrysalis. (*S*, pp. 209-210)

In *The Edible Woman, The Journals of Susanna Moodie, Surfacing*, the "Circe/Mud Poems" in *You Are Happy*, and above all in *Lady Oracle*, Atwood uses elements of the Triple Goddess pattern. Each of these works portrays a woman who "finds herself shut like a moth in a chrysalis." In *The Edible Woman* and *Surfacing* this chrysalis resembles an icy chaste Diana. Marion in *The Edible Woman* remains trapped, like Canadian Rapunzels, within herself. The protagonist of *Surfacing* manages to conceive a child and to prepare herself for transformation from a Diana into a more complete person: to describe her as a Venus, however, is scarcely appropriate. Susanna Moodie embodies each of the traditional three phases. Nevertheless, it is as crone embodying the spirit of this land that Moodie is most impressive. The figure of the Circe/Mud woman in *You Are Happy* ironically reverses the pattern. Instead of

5

a Venus trapped within a Diana or a Hecate, Circe's and the Mud woman's sexuality becomes a trap perceived as evil in the one case and as mindless raw material in the other. Atwood's most intriguing treatment of the Triple Goddess idea is, without doubt, in *Lady Oracle*. Joan Foster is a grotesque parody of a Canadian Rapunzel hiding a lush red-haired Venus inside one hundred pounds of fat. For Joan the "moth in a chrysalis" idea, with its potential for transformation, becomes a travesty when she is forced to dance as a mothball — no butterfly wings for her. As Atwood says of Canadian Diana-Venus-Hecate plots, "the story can also be about the attempts of the buried Venuses and Dianas to get out [of the Hecate chrysalis], to free themselves" (p. 210). And Joan's life is a comic version of this story.

In the concluding chapter of *Survival*, "Jail-Breaks and Recreations," Atwood speculates upon the future of Canadian literature. Her suggestions, while they may prove generally applicable, indicate specific tendencies in her own work. She argues, first of all, that individualistic heroes may not be suited to the Canadian psyche; they are American transplants and do not flourish here. Collective heroes, however, have more potential. The idea of the collective as opposed to individual hero is consistent with Atwood's view of the self, and her heroes — the chief protagonists in her fiction, Susanna Moodie, the voice in many of the poems — should be approached in this light; while they are particularized, especially in the fiction, they are not highly individualized, three-dimensional characters so much as representatives or symbols of social concerns, archetypes and myth. Secondly, Atwood suggests that contemporary writers are exploring ways of breaking free from various stereotypes in order to re-create their experience. The prevalence of this theme in Atwoood's work does not need to be belaboured here. Third, and most important, she emphasizes the need for affirming our experience through acceptance of our duality. In our literature,

> there are elements which... transcend [negativity] — the collective hero, the halting but authentic break-throughs made by characters who are almost hopelessly trapped, the moments of affirmation that neither deny the negative ground nor succumb to it. (*S*, p. 245)

Whether or not violent duality is a viable image for our literature or an accurate reflection of our culture, Margaret Atwood's poetry and fiction dramatize the duplicity of life and the struggle, in words, for an affirmation that neither denies nor succumbs.

6

Chapter II

Tension between Subject and Object

> through eyes
> made ragged by his
> effort, the tension
> between subject and object,
>
> the green
> vision, the unnamed
> whale invaded. (*AC*, p. 39)

Early poems (1959-1965)

A detailed discussion of Margaret Atwood's early published poetry is beyond the scope of this study.[1] However, some points can be made about her work prior to *The Circle Game* (1965) which illustrate development as well as continuity in her writing. Looking at the early verse helps one appreciate the maturity of the rest. In glancing over these poems, many of them scattered in literary journals, others published as chapbooks, certain features strike me as interesting. The six chapbooks, for example, have illustrations, some by Atwood herself, others by Charles Patcher.[2] While the illustrations may not be of great value artistically, they indicate Atwood's interest in the combined effect of poem and picture; the poem appeals to the ear, the illustration to the eye. Atwood achieves a similar double effect, in a more subtle way, in later unillustrated poems where the poem itself demands to be seen on the page as well as heard. *The Journals of Susanna Moodie* (see Chapter III) also incorporates illustrations, this time Atwood collages, accompanying specific poems.

Another recurrent feature is Atwood's apparent liking for poem sequences. Several of her earliest publications comprise a series of separate poems that are related and unified in certain ways. One of the distinctive features of her later books is that each coheres as an imaginative whole, instead of simply offering a collection of individual poems. Atwood often takes legend and myth for subjects in these poem series. Even in early sequences such as "The Seven

Wonders" (1960) and "Avalon Revisited" (1961), she attempts to rework the materials of myth in order to discover fresh meaning.[3] The poems fail for a variety of reasons — ornate style, convoluted syntax, cumbersome rhyme or assonance — but their chief weakness is the clumsy handling of the subject — the myth is undigested and chokes the poem. It would be interesting to trace Atwood's growing skill in handling myth from an early piece like "The Seven Wonders" to the partial success of *Double Persephone* and then to the stunning creation of Mrs. Moodie in the *Journals* or Circe in *You Are Happy*.

In 1961 Hawkshead Press published Atwood's first collection — seven, short, cryptic poems — entitled *Double Persephone*. None of them received authorial sanction in *Selected Poems*, but they are hardly mere juvenilia exhibiting as they do a firm grasp of language, line and image as well being Atwood's first attempt at an interrelated 'book' of poems. The controlling metaphor is that of the original Persephone who, according to the classical myth, was carried off to Hades by Pluto where she must spend half the year. The other half of the year she spends with ther mother, Demeter, thereby figuring forth the death and rebirth of nature.

Atwood's Persephone, variously called "the girl with the gorgon touch," "the idiot girl" and "the dancing girl", is double in many ways. Not only does she represent Winter and Summer, Death and Life, she embodies the deceptive powers of illusion that hide violent realities as in "Persephone Departing":

> The dancing girl's a withered crone:
> Though her deceptive smile
> Lures life from earth, rain from the sky,
> It hides a wicked sickle; while
> Those watching sense the red blood curled
> Waiting, in the centre of her eye;
>
> But the stranger from the hill
> Sees only the bright gleam
> Of a slim woman gathering asphodel,
> And lashes his black team.[4]

According to the myth, Pluto with his black horses captured Persephone as she gathered flowers with her nymphs, but Atwood's "stranger" has clearly been deceived by pleasant appearances and will grab hold of more than he can handle. As Atwood says repeatedly in her work, vision is untrustworthy; perception is relative and partial.

Persephone represents a further duality in this collection, one as important and pervasive as that of illusion and reality. Persephone as natural cycle and as myth embodies the opposing forces of life and art. Certain of the titles suggest this opposition: "Formal Garden," "Pastoral," "Iconic Landscape" and "Chthonic Love." In "Formal Garden" we meet "the girl with the gorgon touch" who turns everything into "marbled flesh" "curved in all-too-perfect grace." The world in "Iconic Landscape" is equally static and dead, sustained by an "idiot girl" with "her cold sun."[5] Persephone is another metaphor for the artist who hypostatizes life in her poems and myths.

The descriptions of the natural cycle, however, do not seem much more reassuring. In "Pastoral," the "amorous shepherd" "dwindles down to spine / And dawdles in the snow alone, / Fiddling a tune across his bone." It is in "Her Song," with its siren overtones, that Persephone distinguishes between art and life — and the alternatives are hardly encouraging:

> There are two kinds of death;
> One rots the breath
> From the urgent bone ...
> The other folds life up
> And slides it through the door ...
>
> Love, you must choose
> Between two immortalities:
> One of earth lake trees
> Feathers of a nameless bird
> The other of a world of glass,
> Hard marble, carven word.

We can choose the natural death of the seasons and organic forms, or the death of artifice where, like a letter, we will land in a "lost garden" of "glass, / Hard marble, carven word." This damned-if-you-do-damned-if-you-don't situation is particularly acute for the artist and becomes a constant pressure in Atwood's verse. The word, paradoxically, is both necessary for artistic life and a trap antithetical to life. As the speaker in "Their Attitudes Differ" will remark, "Please die... so I can write about it" (*PP*, p. 10).

Two *Alphabet* poems published in 1962 reiterate this central Atwood concern with the relationship of art/life and the artist.[6] In "The Witch & The Nightingale," the artist is a witch who entraps

9

living forms, much as "the girl with the gorgon touch" does in *Double Persephone* or, as Circe will do in *You Are Happy*. Thus, the Nightingale cries:

> I am caught, a painted bird
> in a cage of painted words;
> unsay the hook that holds me bound
> and let me splinter
> back beyond all thought and letter

The Witch, of course, argues that her world of artifice is pleasant, an "eden," safe from temporal change and mortality because it is "static." The Nightingale repeats its plea:

> You changed your hut into a palace
> of pallid snow with frozen roses;
> Maker, break your ice of art
> release the sleeping singer
> folded in my golden heart.

The old romantic problem has been reversed. Instead of seeking an escape from change in art, the singer desires life, warmth, and the flow of time. The dilemma is neither new nor, with its echoes of Keats and Yeats, freshly expressed. The images of snow and ice, however, as well as the references to eyes ("I spiked my world upon your eye:") and mirrors ("It is time to drop your mirror"), point forward to important images in Atwood's later work.

The use of voice in both "The Witch & The Nightingale" and its companion piece, "The Whore & The Dove," foreshadows the use of voice in later, more complex and subtle, poems. Both poems are dialogues in which the voices represent opposite or opposing principles. The whore and dove of the second poem speak for physical reality and spirituality respectively. But after the collapse of this Descartean universe in part II of the poem, the two speakers grow beyond their previous limits:

> Past opposites, grasping at thin redemption
> We, the last aspects of a scattered whole
> Must writhe in an imperfect incarnation.

In the later poem, as we shall see, the split voice clearly belongs to one speaker who, as a divided self, particularizes the vague "scattered whole" of this early poem.

In 1963 *Alphabet* published four new Atwood poems which, with the advantage of hindsight, are interesting for thematic and formal reasons. In "The Orphan From Alberta," "Poor Tom" and "Mad Mother Ballad," Atwood constructs extended metaphors of the Canadian landscape. "Poor Tom" is not Shakespeare's "unaccommodated man," but our own unmistakable scene. Image, choice of word, and the abrupt short linear thrust of line, reveal Atwood's emerging powers. It is the energy, apparent in the first part of this poem, that I admire in so many of the later poems:

> Poor Tom
>
> is thatched with straw, and whistles
> when the wind blows;...
>
> he tramples down the cornrows
>
> snagged and crazy as a cedar
> stump; and the earth grows
> out through him, immanent
> in sandy bramble-hair, the chilblained
> bedrock of his jawbone, rough redpine
> of spine[7]

Poor Tom, "snagged and crazy as a cedar / stump," is Atwood's first offering to the long line of Canadian nature monsters which she lists in *Survival*. In later poems, and in *Surfacing*, the speaker or protagonist will internalize this dangerous, crazy nature, thus doing away with the necessity for the creation of a character such as Tom.

Perhaps it is leaning too heavily on an early piece such as this to subject it to further scrutiny, but two further observations might well be made. In the second part of the poem which is set apart parenthetically, the poet asks "(what if some farmer / could force him to be sane...?)" Can man tame this wilderness? The passage is gauche, but Atwood's juxtaposition of nature and culture is a recognizable theme that pervades *The Animals in That Country, The Journals of Susanna Moodie* and *Surfacing*. Trying to force square lines onto curved space will lead inevitably to the progressive insanities of a pioneer; "Poor Tom" will have his revenge. Also, Atwood uses parentheses and a two-part structure in this poem, devices which she develops and refines in order to gain remarkable effects in her later work. In fact, parenthesis and duplistic structure become distinctive features of the later poems.

The fourth poem in the sequence is a small *tour-de-force*. The subject has become a staple in Atwood's canon — sexual role-playing and victimization. But, as with "They Eat Out" (*PP*, p. 5) or "Tricks With Mirrors" (*YAH*, p. 24-28), who wins and who loses is a moot point. The ground is heavily mined and the male, be he Pluto, superman, Odysseus himself, or an "evil Dwarf," had best take care — "Little Nell" is no Snow White:

> Though she's the victim
> Caught by the limp whiplash of
> The hunchbacked rhetorician
> Who goads her terrors with his tongue,
>
> She's an iron maiden
> Inflexible as metal;... (p. 54)

"Fall and All: a Sequence" (1964), "Talismans for Children" (1965), and "Kaleidescopes: Baroque" (1965) elaborate further upon what has already become a basic Atwood theme: in these poems, as in *Double Persephone*, simple opposites embody a more complex and subtle duality.[8] For example, "The Siamese Twins," fourth poem in the "Fall and All" sequence, portrays the duality of sexual love that must be recognized before the lovers can be truly united. "He" and "she" struggle against their bonds,

> Roped in one continual skin
> Their opposite bodies mingled
> And bound by knotted skeins...

without realizing their dilemma:

> Now Love cannot sever
> Their too-single heart
> Though they must tear themselves apart
> To ever come together.

In their facile denial of separateness, "Their too-single heart," these lovers cannot love. A similar predicament expressed in similar images appears in the title sequence of Atwood's most recent volume, *Two-Headed Poems*, where the hapless twins are the founding peoples of this country. In the seventh poem of "Fall and All"/ "The Double Nun" the condition of duality reflects a split within the self, the inside/outside" of the speaker. The nun, or inner self,

                    remains secure,
Safe as a prisoner; while I
Her shadow and her decoy
Must run (that she may hide)

"Talismans for Children" portrays a threatening world of opposites. The children in the poem need protection from the "iron
strangle- / hold" of a society that will change them into robots or
objects. In fact, Atwood portrays the endangered children much as
Blake does in *Songs of Innocence and Experience* where "priests in
black gowns" wait to ensnare and bind their youthful energy. Quite
possibly Blake, via James Reany, influenced both Atwood's interest
in duality and her strange pictures of childhood as a precarious state
constantly threatened from without and needing to protect itself
behind walls. In "Kaleidescopes: Baroque," for example, the child in
her "eight-walled" summerhouse rejects the kaleidescopes which offer her two new eyes to view the world — one provides "enclosed
geometries," the other is "an eye of mirrors." Once again duality is
rejected and with it the vision of "a change, a transformation;" the
child returns to "The circle of her days."

An examination of Atwood's early verse does not reveal the kind
of juvenilia that George Bowering unearthed in his study of Al Purdy; Atwood published few poems comparable to the rhyme,
metre, and diffuse sentiment of Purdy's *The Enchanted Echo*.[9] Her
beginnings were not so much false as tentative and self-conscious.
The themes that have continued to interest Atwood were already present — duality, the tension between art and life, the dilemma of the
artist, problems of role-playing, victimization, the fallibility of
human perception, and of course, portrayal of the Canadian landscape. Her most striking achievement in *The Circle Game* is the formal advance over the earlier work. The most successful poems in
The Circle Game are tightly controlled and economically formed.
The use of language, while not strikingly different, is more precise,
more finely pointed. Above all, Atwood finds a voice in *The Circle
Game* that focuses the disturbing vision and ironic backlash of her
best work. She ceases to write third person poems *about* nature or
victims or artists and locates her point of view within the subject
itself. This discovery of voice is Atwood's great strength. It was a
bold and dangerous discovery, however, because it has led to facile
confusions of the woman with the writer and consequent — often
wilful — misreading of the work.

The Circle Game
(1966)

Margaret Atwood has said that she does not "write books of
poetry as books."[10] At the same time, it is obvious that each of her
books of poetry, from *Double Persephone* on, has an inner logic and
unity, especially thematic, but to some degree structural. The poems
do not appear in a haphazard order. Indeed, I think that one of
Atwood's major contributions to our poetry is that, with others such
as Reaney, Macpherson, and Purdy, she offers us 'books' of poems
instead of miscellanies. This said, however, it is unnecessary and un-
justified to force a Procrustean cookie cutter onto any given collection. Neat pigeon-holing is especially tricky with *The Circle Game*
which carries its own warning about such intrusions in "Letters,
Towards and Away":

> You came easily into my house
> and without being asked
> washed the dirty dishes,...
>
> restoring some kind of
> daily normal order.
>
> Not normal for me: (*CG*, p. 70)

Nevertheless, it is possible to make some general observations
about the shape and movement of the book. *The Circle Game* offers
poems that embody various kinds of vicious circles. The speaker in
the poems, having met with disasters in life, retreats into the self or
sets out into a wilderness in the effort to escape, to break free. The
controlling metaphor is one of journeying, be it under a lake,
through a carpet, across Canada, or simply "to the interior." But the
atmosphere of these highly spatial poems is claustrophobic; the
speaker herself wonders "(have I been / walking in circles again?)."

The opening poem, "This is a Photograph of Me," places the
speaker "in the lake, in the centre / of the picture, just under the surface." And yet the voice seems to be coming from beside the reader
as they observe the snapshot together. The speaker is split, in the
lake and not in it, in the photograph and not in it, drowned but not
drowned. Why? How are we eventually to see her? Learning *how* to
see is the best way to break out of the vicious circles in Atwood's
world. If, however, we have a drowned speaker, it is possible that she
will surface with a special insight — but not before the world down

14

there and the reasons for descent have been told.

In "After the Flood, We," the speaker is clearly aware of the depths of reality while her jaunty companion, "not even knowing / that there has been a flood," slips along on the surfaces of life. The idea that the speaker and her companion inhabit separate worlds recurs frequently. In "The Islands," the speaker appears to accept the necessity for separateness. Elsewhere, separation is threatening. The tenuous position of the people in "After the Flood, We," the sole survivors of a disaster only one of them recognizes, is reiterated in "Spring in the Igloo." Here again, the speaker understands the danger. She has built an ice house for her love so that her lover can rival the sun, but life does not stand still in "glacial innocence":

> and so we are drifting
> into a tepid ocean
> on a shrinking piece of winter...
>
> with ice the only thing
> between us and disaster. (*CG*, p. 48)

Although the impending shock of reality will destroy the frozen lovers, disaster seems necessary as well as inevitable. It is one possible way out of a static situation.

"A Descent Through the Carpet" offers the first detailed description of underwater life. It is a world of "cold jewelled symmetries," of "voracious eater" and "voracious eaten." In this descent into the primordial depths of the self, the dreamer in the poem, like the protagonist in *Surfacing*, discovers not Eden but a world of "total fear." She surfaces abruptly, "beached on the carpet," inside and outside resume their distinct positions, but the knowledge she returns with is less than helpful. She is left with a "sackful of scales," and "remnants of ancestors" and the realization that she has been "dredged up from time" in the midst of conflict. "These wars" become specific in "Eventual Proteus" and "A Meal." In the former, the lovers are reduced to "sparring in the vacant spaces," their voices "abraded with fatigue" and their "bodies wary." In the latter, it is clear that the speaker is emotionally starved by the stalemate. Her body, like Old Mother Hubbard's cupboard, is empty, except for "the necessary cockroach." It comes out at night when it is safe from "your mind's hands that smell / of insecticide and careful soap." Only then can the "furtive insect" gorge itself on the "spilled crumbs of love."

15

In the title poem, "The Circle Game," the speaker defines the "prisoning rhythms" that entrap her and by recognizing her position she is finally able to assert her desire to break free: "I want the circle / broken." In "Camera," she has made good her escape from "your organized instant." Love is impossible in a static world:

> there has been a hurricane
>
> that small black speck
> travelling towards the horizon
> at almost the speed of light
>
> is me (*CG*, p. 46)

The road to freedom and enlightenment is hardly straight, and in the subsequent poems the speaker seems to be as trapped as ever. In "Spring in the Igloo," she knows she is skating on thin ice. In "Migration: C.P.R.," one of the best individual poems in the collection, the speaker and her companion are trapped like Stephen Daedalus in the nets of ancestors and language. Seeking "a place of absolute / unformed beginning," they set out across the country only to find the barriers of language and the past in Vancouver.

"Journey to the Interior" describes a troubled relationship, in which the speaker is almost lost, as in a wilderness. The traditional travelling aids are useless because unfitted for this landscape. The speaker suspects she has been "walking in circles." "Pre-Amphibian" offers a ray of hope. The dominant images, recalling "This is a Photograph of Me" and "Descent through the Carpet," are of submergence in water and sleep. This watery night-life marks a release from the restrictions and perceptions of waking life when we play our vicious circle games:

> released
> from the lucidities of day
> when you are something I can
> trace a line around, with eyes
> cut shapes
> from air, the element
> where we
> must calculate according to
> solidities (*CG*, p. 63)

For a brief while the lovers "blur" together. Then the "merciless sunlight" of morning brings separation because "we / see each other through the / hardening scales of waking." This poem brings together the two major themes of the book — the journeys under water or away from entrapment and the analyses of a variety of confining circles — and isolates limited human perception as the main culprit. Because we cannot *see* properly, we cannot find the drowned speaker in "This is a Photograph of Me," we cannot understand the complex depths of life, we cannot distinguish the reality of a separate human being from the carefully ordered existence we wish to perceive. But how do we learn to see correctly? How do we overcome the alienating one-sidedness of life?

"Against Still Life," by its very title, emphasizes the necessity for movement, life, an attempt at communication. In words that recall "The Circle Game" and point forward to *You Are Happy*, the speaker asserts, *I want* — "I want / anything you can say / in the sunlight"[11] — "in the sunlight" because we are not "preamphibians" and must learn to live in the light of day.

The closest Atwood comes to answering the question of how we break the circle is in "A place: Fragments." The poem turns on the question of sight. If we are too close, all we will see is fragments; "We must move back" to acquire perspective — on ourselves, on others, on any landscape. In fact, we must find another way of perceiving that is better than sight:

> An other sense tugs at us:
> we have lost something,
> some key to these things ...
>
> something not lost or hidden
> but just not found yet
>
> that informs, holds together
> this confusion, this largeness
> and dissolving:
>
> not above or behind
> or within it, but one
> with it: an
>
> identity:
> something too huge and simple
> for us to see. (*CG*, p. 76)

Once confining circles are broken, one is left floundering. An order is needed that does not cripple life, reducing it to circle games. Whatever that order will be, it will be too large "for us to see."

Atwood apparently agrees with McLuhan that the visual sense isolates objects in space.

In "The Explorers" and "The Settlers," the poet brings us full circle, on the one hand recalling by image and point of view the drowned speaker of the opening poem, on the other hand returning us to essentials, perhaps to new beginnings. In the first poem "we" are "the two skeletons," all that is left of the "wary" combatants of "Eventual Proteus." In "The Settlers," the two skeletons are "so intermixed, one / carcass" that they have grown new flesh. Certainly, the speaker in the poem who has become "one with" the land is not trapped or alone. In an extended metaphor of body as landscape we feel the freedom of this voice:

> children run, with green
> smiles, (not knowing
> where) across
> the fields of our open hands. (*CG*, p. 80)

Atwood is working here with a myth similar to that in *Surfacing*. The self, trapped in many senses, and struggling to break free into an existence that is harmonious, independent, yet related to others, must return to the primitive roots of being, the elemental life of water and earth, in order to begin again. The next phase of the journey is problematic, but this much seems clear: the key to success will be too large "for us to see."

One of the most remarkable features of *The Circle Game* is the formal control of individual poems. Most poems have a two-part structure through which Atwood achieves stunning and disturbing doubling effects. The second part of the poem often reflects the first part, but the mirror image will be distorted. The dynamic of these poems exists in the juxtaposition of subject and reflection which forces us to question the authenticity and the reliability of our own senses. I frequently feel that I have been led through an innocuous gateway into a labyrinth of mirrors which distorts former perceptions and responses. Nothing is certain except the challenge in Atwood's hall of mirrors. The element of doubling, moreover, is not confined to the structure of certain poems; it is apparent in voice, in image, in line and, consequently, in theme.

In "Man With A Hook," "The City Planners," "Spring in the Igloo" or "The Settlers" the shift is indicated simply with "But." Like a very long sentence, or the octave and sestet of a sonnet, the poem changes direction with a sudden revelation that explodes the preceding view of events. In other poems such as "Winter Sleepers," or "Playing Cards," the shift is indicated as a change in perspective from inside to outside. In "An Attempted Solution For Chess Problems," Atwood retains the "but" in parentheses, "(but)," and "A Descent Through the Carpet" develops through several inside/outside parallels.

"This is a Photograph of Me" achieves its special shock through a double structure as well. The second part, an apparently offhand parenthetical remark, turns the description of a snapshot inside out:

This is a Photograph of Me

It was taken some time ago.
At first it seems to be
a smeared
print: blurred lines and grey flecks
blended with the paper;...

(The photograph was taken
the day after I drowned.

I am in the lake, in the center
of the picture, just under the surface....

but if you look long enough,
eventually
you will be able to see me.) (*CG*, p. 11)

The first point to make, I feel, is that the poem must be *seen* for its full effect; Atwood's poetry is highly visual. The controlling metaphor of the poem is visual as well, for the eye moves down the page and around and into a photograph simultaneously. At the same time, a first-person voice is clearly speaking. Stranger still, the speaker has drowned! Like so many of Atwood's poems, this one must be seen on the page, yet it is spoken; it is visual and aural/oral, playing off the expectations of one against the effects of the other.

The poem questions our perceptual methods. In the first part we are shown an object which is described realistically; this is easy enough to see. The second part of the poem distorts the first reality, while apparently continuing a matter-of-fact description, by splitting the focus. How can we see the disembodied speaker and, if we do, what will we learn, what will happen to the neatly ordered surfaces of reality? A similar tactic is present in "Journey to the Interior" where the equation of self with landscape and the abrupt shift from

19

external verifiable reality to private distortion of reality, create the sense of acute uneasiness and shock. The division of the poem is marked in terms that epitomize the purpose for the doubled metaphoric structure in so many Atwood poems: "There are similarities / I notice" — "There are differences / of course." The "of course," similar to the "but" in some poems or the parentheses in "This is a Photograph of Me," imparts a casual note to a dramatic, unexpected development in the poem. The similarities between the two parts of these poems provide the springboard for a leap into astonishing and threatening differences.

The title poem, "The Circle Game," is the most important single poem in the book. On the one hand, it offers an explicit analysis of the problems of entrapment; on the other, it echoes or foreshadows several other poems, most notably "Tricks With Mirrors" from *You Are Happy*, and elements of the protagonists' predicament in each of the novels. It is also a beautifully crafted poem.

The poem develops in terms of four main images of stasis or entrapment that one finds repeatedly in Atwood's work, rooms, maps, mirrors and circles. The children going "round and round" initiate the circle image. But we must not "mistake this / tranced moving for joy," for "there is no joy in it." In part VII the lovers become trapped in the circle, "arm in arm," like the children in part I. The speaker blames her lover for the vicious circle of their lives because he apparently controls the "closed rules" of their games. The cycles of the seasons offer no respite; summer simply brings out the children "singing / the same song" which, in turn, becomes "a round cage of glass" spun by their "thread-thin / insect voices." The speaker, finally, wants to break "your prisoning rhythms" of song, dance, love.

The lovers are equally entrapped by mirrors:

Being with you,
here, in this room

is like groping through a mirror
whose glass has melted
to the consistency
of gelatin (*CG*, p. 36)

The mirror is not simply one of the "many mirrors here... in this room." It is the people themselves who refuse to be either "an exact reflection" or separate beings. Inaccurate reflection distorts personal identity so that one cannot see clearly either oneself or another person. Often the man looks past her to his own reflection, ignoring her presence, and, in part VII, the children recur, wheeling and singing "in the mirrors of this room."

Before I turn to the room imagery, it is interesting to note the map images. The map provides one of the most striking and violent images in the poem. The speaker remembers that her lover likes "(not making but)" tracing maps in order to hold things "in their proper places." He is methodical, uninventive, interested only in order, not discovery. Predictably, the speaker becomes a map that he will trace and pin down:

> So now you trace me
> like a country's boundary ...
>
> and I am fixed, stuck
> down on the outspread map
> of this room, of your mind's continent ...
>
> transfixed
> by your eyes'
> cold blue thumbtacks (*CG*, p. 40)

His solipsism reduces her to a wrinkle in his skin or an aspect of his "mind's continent." Eyes as "cold blue thumbtacks" is one of Atwood's most effective, direct images for the dangers of visual perception.

Rooms are not only important images but an organizing principle within the poem. Through much of the poem the lovers are enclosed in a room listening to the children outside and the noises from another room. The room is hardly a sanctuary. Like the useless fort that the children explore, it represents the claustrophobia and monotony of this relationship. It is one room like many others — "the place of our defences." *This* room, one senses, is *this* relationship as the speaker feels herself reduced to nothing more than an "obsolete fort / pulled inside out" — obsolete because, like the weapons from the children's fort now preserved in glass cases "indoors", there is no longer anything much worth defending.

The question of rooms and forts, indoors and outdoors, points to the structure of the poem. It has seven parts but the first four move carefully back and forth between "the children on the lawn" and "here, in this room." Parts one and three describe the children while two and four describe the lovers. Try reading parts one and three, two and four consecutively. Atwood, however, has a surprise in store

21

of much the same kind that pertains in the poems with obvious double structures. Parts five, six and seven bring the two poles of the poem gradually together, reflecting back, in the process, upon the first four sections of the poem. The children, their games, and their fort are a mirror for the couple in the room. This reflected image, unlike the gelatinous distortion in part II, is instructive. In part five, the lovers themselves move outside to "walk ... along / the earthworks." In part six, the speaker realizes that she and her lover play childish games posing, playing roles, playing parlour games or "a game of envy." In the final section of the poem the analogy of children and couple is clear: the children wheel "in the mirrors of this room"; "this casual bed ... is / their grassy lawn." Fusing images from the preceding parts of the poem, outside and inside merge to reveal a terrifyingly accurate image of this childish, violent, destructive game of love. The speaker can now see clearly:

> I want to break
> these bones, your prisoning rhythms
>   (winter,
>   summer)
> all the glass cases,
>
> erase all maps,
> crack the protecting
> eggshell of your turning
> singing children:
>
> I want the circle
> broken. (*CG*, p. 44)

The two most fundamental themes in *The Circle Game* are those of entrapment and duality. Atwood explores experience and presents her dilemmas in terms of opposites or contradictions. For example, "This is a Photograph of Me," "After the Flood, We," "The City Planners," or "Pre-Amphibian," suggest the conflict between the surfaces and depths of reality. We keep the surfaces of life neatly ordered like city planners in a desperate effort to ignore the chaos beneath. Yet, it is just possible that descent will issue in renewal. In any case, as the speaker in "Spring in the Igloo" realizes, immersion is inevitable.

Our problem, and Atwood's, is epistemological. Because we are afraid of what we partially perceive beneath the surface, we insist upon "still life" and "daily normal order." This obsession, ironically, leads to its own form of insanity; we prescribe roles for ourselves and others that distort life and entrap us. Our vision consists of "cold blue thumbtacks;" our knowledge, like our maps, is unreliable, our language obsolete. We walk in circles. In order to break free we must take the plunge seeking "An other sense." The breaking away is itself painful and threatening; the first impression is that we and others are diminished:

> Shrunk by my disbelief
> you cannot raise
> the green gigantic skies, resume
> the legends of your disguises: (*CG*, p. 31)

We must learn to see without stopping life like the camera-man in "Camera" with his glass eye. This problem of stasis and perception is especially acute for the artist. Atwood probes the tension between art and life in "Some Objects of Wood and Stone," and "Against Still Life." Against the inevitable pull towards stasis of a poem which interrupts and shapes the flow of life, Atwood pits the energy of her language, images, and poetic forms in hopes that these will jolt our perceptions causing us to see things upside-down or inside-out. Her poems are crafty mirrors.

The Animals in That Country
(1968)

The Circle Game explores the individual's perception of herself and others; *The Animals in That Country* explores the ways individuals relate and respond to their environments, the ones they create and the ones they find. Where the atmosphere in *The Circle Game* is deliberately claustrophobic and solipsistic, *The Animals in That Country* anatomizes extreme self-centredness.

The controlling metaphor of the collection is that of land as self or country as body. In certain ways *Animals* looks back to the last three poems in *The Circle Game*, picking up the associations of human body as landscape as well as the animistic point of view (which we find again in *You Are Happy*). In certain key poems of *Animals* the speaking voice is that of the land itself. Generally speaking, however, I find *Animals* a less rewarding book. Too often the poems become abstract or vague or simply sag. The level of intensity and excitement is not sustained. At the same time, another *Circle Game* would be too much of a good thing. Atwood does offer

23

more varied types of poems here, for example, the meditative-lyric poem "River," narratives like "Progressive Insanities of a Pioneer," as well as the poetic bombshells one associates with her, such as "More and More." The main distinction I want to make between this book and the earlier one, however, is not simply evaluative. Poems like "More and More" and "The Surveyors" are very fine; the point is that they develop in a linear fashion, gradually opening up their meanings whereas the excitement in so many of the poems in *The Circle Game* derives from their duplistic structure.

In terms of theme and point of view, the poems fall into three categories. As the title and title poem suggest, there are two countries, one is man-made, unnatural, artificial, ordered, the other is not. Axiomatically, one is known, the other is not:

> Axiom: you are a sea.
> Your eye-
> lids curve over chaos ...
>
> Soon you will be
> all earth: a known
> land, a country (*AC*, p. 69)

What this poem does not reveal is that the known country of order is, as often as not, dead; only "the other country" (*AC*, p. 58), lives. One group of poems describes the known dead country; a second group describes the country of living things. In between are a small number of especially significant poems that present problems of human response to environment.

The opening poem, "Provisions," signals our departure on a fresh Atwood journey, a journey for which we are dismally prepared:

> so here we are, in thin
> raincoats and rubber boots
>
> on the disastrous ice, the wind rising,
>
> nothing in our pockets (*AC*, p. 1)

The "disastrous ice" recalls the precarious situation of the lovers from "Spring in the Igloo" in *The Circle Game*. The presence in our pockets of "small white filing-cards / printed with important facts" is ominous; of what conceivable use will a filing-card mentality be in "the other country"? "The Animals in That Country" suggests some of the differences between countries: in Egypt, England, Spain and

24

Northern Europe, the animals are human, they die elegant deaths; here, the animals are animals and "Their deaths are not elegant." I find it hard to decide where the animals are better off. In either place they die. But from the human point of view "that country" is comfortable, known, humanized through myth and "forests thickened with legend."

"The Landlady" and "A Fortification" offer sharp insights into the terrors of life in a country of order and "raucous fact." The landlady, "a raw voice," "a bulk, a knot / swollen in space," traps the speaker in space, controlling her life, renting out time, circumventing her escapes. The landlady is a static reality, "immutable ... solid as bacon." In order to survive in such a world, one must become invulnerable. Therefore, "A Fortification" describes the body as "a metal spacesuit":

> I have armed myself, yes I am safe: safe:
> the grass can't hurt me.
> My senses swivel like guns in their fixed sockets:
> I am barriered from leaves and blood. (*AC*, p. 16)

The speaker in the poem has cut herself off from the natural world. She is like the protagonist in *Surfacing*, cut off from her true self and aware of another self with "real skin, real hair" who has vanished "back to the lost forest of being vulnerable" (AC, p. 16). In a later poem, "Roominghouse, winter," the speaker realizes the terrible danger to life in this country:

> We must resist. We must refuse
> to disappear
>
> I said, In exile
> survival
> is the first necessity. (*AC*, p. 29)

About the only positive thing to be said for the speaker in these poems is that she is trying to hang on long enough to be able to break out of deathscapes. Unlike her companion in "Roominghouse, winter," who acquiesces — "Nobody ever survives" — the speaker is at least in "Victim Position # Three."

In "At the tourist centre in Boston," Atwood approaches the problems of distortion / truth, surfaces / depths, order / chaos, space / time, from another angle. The whole of Canada is trapped inside the tourist's perception, reduced to a "map with red dots for the cities" and a series of ten snapshots. Maps and snapshots are constant Atwood images for stasis and entrapment. Here, they symbolize the false surfaces and stereotypes through which we *think* we see reality:

> Whose dream is this, I would like to know:
> is this a manufactured
> hallucination, a cynical fiction, a lure
> for export only? (*AC*, p. 18)

This question, in conjunction with the final questions of the poem, pinpoints the danger inherent in controlled one-sided vision: how do we distinguish reality from hallucination, or worse still, dreamer from dream? If this "country under glass" is the truth, then one's own perception of a living reality is nothing but a "private mirage." If the image of a country does not reflect reality, then the inhabitants will not know the answer to "Where is here?"; "If a country or a culture lacks... mirrors it has no way of knowing what it looks like; it must travel blind" (*S*, p. 16).

Still pursuing the contrast between living reality and static reductive space, Atwood offers a fresh example of deathscape in "A Night in the Royal Ontario Museum":

> Who locked me
>
> into this crazed man-made
> stone brain
>   where the weathered
> totempole jabs a blunt
> finger at the byzantine
> mosaic dome (*AC*, p. 20)

A sign announces "YOU ARE HERE," but "here" is nothing more than the mausoleum for modern man's obsession to collect, to label, to ossify history and life. In the museum, objects wrenched from their contexts and fixed in time, symbolize death — "the mind's / deadend, The roar of the bone- / yard."

In "The Totems" and "Elegy for the Giant Tortoises," Atwood meditates upon the cost of a filing-card and museum mentality. "The Animals in That Country" offers us a picture of a world humanized where animals are really people; for the humans this is comfortable. If pursued to its logical conclusion, however, this shaping of the world devitalizes it, thereby cutting us off from vital sources of life and leaving us with masks and relics in museums. In "The Totems," foreshadowing Susanna Moodie's nearly found knowledge in *The Journals*, the speaker asks why the mind is "crowded with hollow totems / ... without motion?" The answer — "I fell asleep and forgot them." We turn "blind eyes" to our environments because we do not know how to see what is there, and it is only right that "The animals" abandon us "leaving their masks behind." "Elegy for the giant tortoises" is less metaphoric. Like other living forms the tortoises are heading for extinction in museum catalogue and exhibit:

> where the brittle gods are kept,
> the relics of what we have destroyed,
> our holy and obsolete symbols. (*AC*, p. 23)

Perhaps the greatest crime, as far as Atwood is concerned, is the rejection of responsibility. She argues for the evil of passive innocence in *Survival* and *Surfacing*, and in her conversation with Graeme Gibson she describes violence and passivity as equally futile:

> you know, you can define yourself as innocent and get killed, or you can define yourself as a killer and kill others. I think there has to be a third thing again; the ideal would be somebody who would neither be a killer or a victim, who could achieve some kind of harmony with the world, which is a productive or creative harmony, rather than a destructive relationship towards the world.
>
> (Gibson, p. 27)

Hints of the "third thing" are rare in Atwood's work, but in "It is dangerous to read newspapers," the speaker blames her passive innocence for causing evil and destruction in terms recalling "the girl with gorgon touch" in *Double Persephone*:

> I am the cause, I am a stockpile of chemical
> toys, my body
> is a deadly gadget,
> I reach out in love, my hands are guns,
> my good intentions are completely lethal. (*AC*, p. 30)

"Even [her] / passive eyes" are guilty. This is the lowest point in *The Animals in That Country*. Here the speaker realizes that she is responsible for the horrors and sterility of the ordered, man-made, unnatural environment, but she does not know what to do about it. By simply recognizing the situation, however, she has taken a first step.

The next group of poems that I want to consider is devoted to presenting "this country" from various points of view. In "The Surveyors," nature reclaims its own territory with an ineluctable pressure. Those who chart and measure a given territory enter blindly, "clearing / their trail of single reason /... through a land where geometries are multiple" (*AC*, p. 4). But nature has the power to transform and obliterate their intrusions through "the gradual pressures of endless / green on the eyes" until the arrogant marks of the surveyor are meaningless,

> red vestiges of an erased
> people, a broken
> line (*AC*, p. 4)

In "Progressive Insanities of a Pioneer," Atwood presents the confrontation of Man and Nature, of straight lines and "multiple geometries," from the pioneer's perspective. Though more violent, the outcome is the same.

"Notes from various pasts" presents the artist's struggle with a language that is becoming increasingly difficult to understand or use. Words are the artist's entry into the world of living forms; they are themselves magic "once-living / and phosphorescent meanings." But in metaphors recalling "A Descent through the Carpet" (*CG*, pp. 21-23), the poet depicts the dilemma of the sophisticated, rational being who has surfaced from the primordial depths of time or the imagination and, in the process, damaged the visionary text. The artist fishing for "messages / from a harsher level," has lost the ability to decipher them. Thus, Atwood calls into question the creative act itself. Language, like fish, cannot be trapped in nets, hauled to the surface, and live. But how are we to know the living country if we cannot speak of it? Paradoxically, the poem both describes the "electric wisdom" of the poet at the same time as it laments the apparently destructive poetic process. The question of the role of the artist and the nature of art is central to Atwood. She returns to it frequently, always testing the power of art to create life against its inescapable threat to life.

"Backdrop addresses cowboy" allows the 'other', the landscape, to speak for itself. Mid-way in the poem, one realizes where the voice is coming from:

> I am the horizon
> you ride towards, the thing you can never lasso
>
> I am also what surrounds you:...
>
> I am the space you desecrate
> as you pass through. (*AC*, p. 51)

"You" is the cowboy in full republican regalia, the heroic stereotypic American, "innocent as a bathtub / full of bullets." He is straight out of "High Noon," but he also represents the cardboard man-made world which denies or abuses what is actually out there. He is both the American, and the American within us, which Atwood caricatures so devastatingly in *Surfacing*; he is the reductive, destructive point of view. "A Voice" personifies "the other country" as "he." He is "part of the grass"; the sun shines "on the blades of his hands." "We" do not belong. Like the cowboy, "we" are separate, artificial, almost a mirage "across / his field of vision." Being irrelevant, we are quickly obliterated.

The last six poems in the collection offer further perspectives on "this country" — the unknown, living land. In "The Reincarnation of Captain Cook," the Captain himself makes a plea for a new kind of exploration in a territory undiscovered. "The eyes raise / tired monuments" while maps and atlases are hindrances in the search for fresh beginnings, or in the attempt to discover "a new land cleaned of geographies." The speaker in "Sundew" comes close to seeing the landscape through a participation in it; she becomes one with water, weeds, and submerged branches. As so often in Atwood, water is the potent element that makes vision possible.

The final four poems extend the idea of "other country" from natural landscape to human territory. Mind and body are described in terms of tree and river, ice and wilderness, sun and universe. The analogy of human and natural in "I was reading a scientific article" suggests the harmonious relationship of two people — a rare occurrence with Atwood — who marvel at and accept the complete mysterious phenomenon of separate living selves:

> You rest on me and my shoulder holds
>
> your heavy unbelievable

29

skull, crowded with radiant
suns, a new planet, the people
submerged in you, a lost civilization
I can never excavate:

my hands trace the contours of a total
universe, its different
colours, flowers, its undiscovered
animals, violent or serene

its other air
its claws

its paradise rivers (*AC*, p. 65)

Here there is no pastiche, no artificiality. Here is a world that cannot
be fully known, summarized on filing cards, locked away in
museums, charted or surveyed. The sense of acceptance and trust —
"You rest on me and my shoulder holds" — of an almost sacred
mystery encompassing duality, makes this poem one of the most
moving, positive poems in the Atwood canon. The speaker does not
emphasize the vulnerable fragility of the moment, but its power.
Thematically, this is the high point of *The Animals in That Country*,
the reality longed for, yet undiscovered in preceding poems. Not until
the end of *You Are Happy* does Atwood again capture such harmony.

Resting between the thematic poles of that country and this
country are "Attitudes towards the mainland," "River," "Astral
Traveller" and "Progressive insanities of a pioneer," poems that
delineate the ambivalence of human response to environment. The
country of museum, map, and backdrop can terrify in its sterility.
The country of green suns and "undiscovered / animals," however,
challenges our very existence, our sanity. The speaker in "Attitudes
towards the mainland," cannot convince her companion to trust, to
accept anything but solidity. And since solidity, or certainty, is an illusion created by "the edges of / my argument, the square white
screen," he is unable to believe in reality — safety consists in pictures of life, not in living. The problem here is essentially fear; ac-
customed to surfaces, we are afraid to let go lest we drown in "the
arid blizzard / in the water, the white suffocation, the snow" (*AC*, p.
9). Here, as in *The Journals of Susanna Moodie* or the conclusion of
Surfacing with the protagonist poised on the edge of risk and trust,
Atwood recalls Eliot's warning in *The Wasteland*:

Datta: what have we given?
My friend, blood shaking my heart
The awful daring of a moment's surrender
Which an age of prudence can never retract
By this, and this only, we have existed[12]

Only by releasing our "numbed grasp on the gunwale" and daring to go down can we hope to surface reborn in "This country."

In "Progressive insanities of a pioneer," the solipsism that proclaims the self as centre, defining all around it, is destroyed by the "green vision" of this country. Whether or not the destruction is fortunate, it is apparently inevitable. The pioneer who settles this country, or anyone who asserts his dominance over an unknown territory, invites disaster if he ignores the separate existence of his surroundings. Each of the seven short sections of the poem portrays successive defeats. The pioneer is deluded to begin with; misunderstanding the surrounding absence, he screams, "Let me out!" He imposes his order upon the land though unable to understand its language. Desperate to set up fences behind which he will be safe in his un-natural world, at night he fears that "everything / is getting in." To his claim that "This country" is "not order / but the absence of order" the forest replies that it is "an ordered absence."

Through the image of the ark, recalling "Attitudes towards the mainland," the poet explains why the pioneer-type will fail:

If he had known unstructured
space is a deluge
and stocked his log house-
boat with all the animals

even the wolves ·

he might have floated. (*AC*, p. 38)

Through ignorance and fear, he sets up limits that divide and exclude. Atwood's pioneer is a perfect embodiment of Frye's "garrison mentality." He is Blake's Newton with single vision. He is a Noah whose ark excludes animals, vision, totems, part of the self. He insists upon seeing the surface of the land as solid, denying the depth of experience. Nature takes its revenge, significantly, in terms of perception,

31

                            and in the end
through eyes
made ragged by his
effort, the tension
between subject and object,

the green
vision, the unnamed
whale invaded. (*AC*, p. 39)

  Because the pioneer refuses to see what is really out there, he is
unable to understand his own position. Paradoxically his defeat comes
from within as much as from without — his mind gives up the struggle to enforce an alien order upon the external world. Given the context of this poem, however, as part of a progressive harmony in *The
Animals in That Country*, I do not think the "green vision" is merely destructive as, for example, the "great flint" in Earle Birney's
"Bushed."[13] Atwood implies that this invasion is a necessary step
towards establishing a harmonious alternative to the adversary positions of that country / this country, and killer/victim, or "the tension / between subject and object." How we resolve this tension in
order to establish the ideal "third thing" that Atwood described in
the Gibson interview, or whether we must be satisfied with the blind
"daring of a moment's surrender," are central questions in the next
collection, *The Journals of Susanna Moodie*.

Chapter III

Two Immortalities

Love, you must choose
Between two immortalities:
One of earth lake trees
Feathers of a nameless bird
The other of a world of glass,
Hard marble, carven word.

"Her Song" (*DP*)

The Journals of Susanna Moodie
(1970)

The Journals of Susanna Moodie is Atwood's major poetic achievement to date. It is a compelling articulation of a Canadian myth and a dramatic incarnation of our past. For these reasons alone, the *Journals* is already a Canadian classic. In the *Journals* Atwood speaks, as much with her own voice as she does with Moodie's, of her deepest concerns with self-perception and national identity. The *Journals* is a stunning fusion of personal vision and moral dilemma with cultural perspective, fully particularized in the persona of Susanna Moodie and Atwood has given it her own endorsement by including it, *in toto*, in *Selected Poems*.

Her "Afterword" to the book explains the design and purpose of the work. The idea of the Moodie poems came in a dream and later, in reading Moodie's *Roughing It in The Bush* and *Life in the Clearings*, she was impressed by the peculiar split personality of Mrs. Moodie.[1] Atwood felt that Mrs. Moodie, "divided down the middle," well symbolized the national schizophrenia; Mrs. Moodie is the archetypal Canadian immigrant, choosing to come here yet preferring somewhere else, perversely loyal yet patronizing, and never able to fully inhabit or know this immense land. It is typical of Atwood, however, to portray our national schizophrenia not simply as illness or weakness, but as our greatest potential strength — accepted and controlled it provides the wisdom of double vision. In fact, the beauty of the *Journals* consists in part, of the convincing ease with which Atwood moves from Mrs. Moodie's schizophrenia to her final acceptance of "the reality of the country she is in, and ... the inescapable doubleness of her own vision" (*JSM*, p. 63), always suggesting that this is what *we* can and should do. For, if we choose to stay in this country that is "so easy to leave ... we are still choosing a violent duality" (*JSM*, p. 62).

In *The Journals of Susanna Moodie*, we have another Atwood voyage or journey in which discovery of self and of place are synonymous. The cryptic prefacing poem emphasizes the importance of perception for this voyage:

> I take this picture of myself
> and with my sewing scissors
> cut out the face.
>
> Now it is more accurate:
>
> where my eyes were,
> every-
> thing appears

Visual perception limits and excludes. Inner vision alone leads to a full understanding of self and "every- / thing." The "I" of the poem is ostensibly Moodie but, as Atwood explains in the "Afterword," she wrote Part III after finding a "little-known photograph of Susanna Moodie as a mad-looking and very elderly lady" (*JSM*, p. 63). The voice, then, works back to Atwood as well as on to Moodie; it is through Atwood that Moodie speaks — through Moodie that Atwood speaks.

The first of the three Journals, 1832-1840, portrays the first years of Mrs. Moodie's life in Upper Canada from her arrival until her move from the bush to the town of Belleville. Journal I presents Moodie's direct experience of this land from the initial confusion and terror, to partial accommodation. The first two poems, "Disembarking at Quebec" and "Further Arrivals," present her alienation. She is unable to see this land as freedom. Looking for some familiar landmark, some object with which she can identify, she is baffled:

> The moving water will not show me
> my reflection.
>
> The rocks ignore.

I am a word
in a foreign language. (*JSM*, p. 11)

She is foreign, incongruous in this landscape. Quite simply, she does not belong. In "Further Arrivals" she is still incapable of overcoming her separateness from the wilderness. Though she realizes, in desperation, that she must do so: "I need wolf's eyes to see / the truth." Unfortunately, to belong here involves the destruction of the former self before new perceptions grow, and because the abandonment of the old and familiar for something strange and new is terrifying, she resists:

I refuse to look in a mirror.

Whether the wilderness is
real or not
depends on who lives there. (*JSM*, p. 13)

Perhaps, if she refuses to look at herself or acknowledge the reality of the wilderness, she will be safe from change and able to assert her British gentlewoman's ascendence over this country.

Things have progressed by the time of "The Planters." Now Moodie knows that the men "deny the ground they stand on," thinking only of the future. She also knows that this future is an "illusion solid to them as a shovel," and that if they were really to see their surroundings, the wilderness, like "the unnamed / whale" in "Progressive Insanities of a Pioneer" (*AC*), would overwhelm them. She knows because she has already been "surrounded, stormed, broken / in upon" by her perception of this land. From this acknowledgement she moves slowly towards her capitulation. For example, in "The Wereman," the power of nature to transform perception takes on frightening yet exciting proportions. She wonders whether the surfaces we see of each other are not camouflage or our own self-centred images that, in fact, hide the real wilderness within. In "Paths and Thingscape," she is still wondering when she will feel accepted by the landscape, "when will be / that union and each / thing ... will without moving move / around me / into its place". The implication is that she fully recognizes the separate existence of nature and would like to be a part of it.

In "The Two Fires," she describes her first experience of doubleness. The poem itself is double, juxtaposing inside and outside, contrasting the "logic of windows" with melting shapelessness or the "white chaos" of nature, in ways that recall many of the poems from *The Circle Game*. What Moodie perceives is the ambivalence of house and nature:

> Two fires in-
> formed me,
>
> (each refuge fails
> us; each danger
> becomes a haven)
>
> left charred marks
> now around which I
> try to grow (*JSM*, p. 23)

By splitting "in- / formed" Atwood emphasizes the knowledge Moodie acquires as well as the fact that she has incorporated the duality of this experience within her.

The last two poems in Journal I present a Susanna Moodie whose perception of herself has gradually been transformed by the pressure of "earth and the strong waters." In "Looking in a Mirror," she realizes that the sun has stained her "its barbarous colour." She is, at least, looking in a mirror, no longer afraid (as she was in "Further Arrivals") to confront what may appear there. Unfortunately, she is not yet sure how to place what she sees in her mirror except that her reflected face contradicts her former perception of herself. In "Departure from the Bush," it is sadly apparent that Moodie has not quite completed her journey of discovery. Likening herself to an ark, an image that recalls the warning from "Progressive Insanities of a Pioneer" (*AC*), she knows she has not yet allowed all the animals, "even the wolves," to enter:

> I was not ready
> altogether to be moved into
>
> They could tell I was
> too heavy: I might
> capsize;
>
> I was frightened
> by their eyes (green or
> amber) glowing out from inside me (*JSM*, pp. 26-27)

Just at this point, historically and psychologically, she leaves the bush for Belleville:

There was something they almost taught me
I came away not having learned. (*JSM*, p. 27)

Although she comes away "not having learned," the situation is not altogether lost. She continues to grow around these vivid experiences of the bush until she can speak in the double voice of culture and nature.[2]

The poems in "Journal II 1840-1871" are written from a different perspective. Instead of immediate experience, these poems are meditations, reflections upon the years in the bush, and dreams. "Death of a Young Son by Drowning" is one of Atwood's simplest and most moving poems. Without hysteria or sentimentality she captures Moodie's grief and loss:

They retrieved the swamped body,

cairn of my plans and future charts,
with poles and hooks
from among the nudging logs....

After the long trip I was tired of waves.
My foot hit rock. The dreamed sails
collapsed, ragged.

I planted him in this country
like a flag. (*JSM*, p. 31)

Illusion shattered, Moodie must accept the reality of this land, but in doing so she courageously transforms defeat into a kind of victory. Through her loss she can become a part of this land, assert her claim to it: "I planted him in this country / like a flag."

"The Immigrants" and "1837 War in Retrospect" have specific historical relevance. In the first, Moodie describes the plight of immigrants coming here as she did, only to confront illness, poverty, hardship, and the intransigence of "an unknown land." Without a new dream to supercede the past they idealize Europe:

the old countries recede, become
perfect, thumbnail castles preserved
like gallstones in a glass bottle, the
towns dwindle upon the hillsides
in a light paperweight-clear. (*JSM*, p. 32)

The problem is typical. It happens today — yet another manifestation of "violent duality," the pull of here and there, in Canada. In the second poem, "1837 War in Retrospect," Moodie reflects upon the flow of history, "rolling itself up in your head / at one end and unrolling at the other" (*JSM*, p. 35). When one is close to the event one sees it in a certain light, but the passing of time alters and confuses the significance. The Moodies, of course, helped to suppress the rebellion. To them it was just that, an insurrection supported by "Yankee" Republicans, and aimed at overthrowing British government. As Atwood points out in her "Afterword," Moodie later came to feel that the 1837 Rebellion was good for Canada. Certainly, it encouraged solidarity and an awareness of common goals.

Interspersed with these reflective poems are three dream poems. Although Moodie has long left the bush behind, she still inhabits it, or it inhabits her, in her dreams. The life that she re-experiences in "Dream I: The Bush Garden" is violent, repulsive:

> In the dream I could
> see down through the earth, could see
> the potatoes curled
> like pale grubs in the soil
> the radishes thrusting down
> their fleshy snouts, the beets
> pulsing like slow amphibian hearts (*JSM*, p. 34)

But even more emphatic is the surging vitality of the bush garden where the plants "come up blood" — their own and the settler's. "Dream 2: Brian the Still-Hunter," involves her memory of a hunter who felt one with his prey:

> but every time I aim, I feel
> my skin grow fur
> my head heavy with antlers
> and during the stretched instant
> the bullet glides on its thread of speed
> my soul runs innocent as hooves. (*JSM*, p. 36)[3]

This sense of unity between hunter and hunted is a frequent element in James Dickey's poetry and the comparison is instructive. For Dickey the union is an aid to the hunter or a way of absorbing animal vitality. But as Atwood presents her vision of union through Moodie, it becomes as destructive of the hunter as the hunted. Brian says "I die more often than many." Indeed, the moral perspective he maintains causes an early attempt at suicide and, the poem implies, a second attempt probably succeeds. In "Dream 3: Night Bear Which Frightened Cattle," the memory of the bear takes on a reality "heavier than real," more solid than dream or imagination, because she perceives it as embodying "all terror." Within the context of Journal II, these three dream poems illustrate the internalizing of the wilderness and prepare the way for "The Double Voice." As Moodie ages, she grows, paradoxically, back towards the bush she left; it is as much a part of her as the civilization of towns and cities.

In both "The Deaths of the Other Children" and "The Double Voice," Moodie contemplates her life thus far. The first poem suggests that she has *accepted* death as a return to the soil. Her arms, eyes, words and "disintegrated children" have already joined the "black- / berries and thistles": "They catch at my heels with their fingers" (*JSM*, p. 41). Her relationship to this land has changed dramatically from the first poem where she was "a word / in a foreign language" (*JSM*, p. 11).

"The Double Voice" marks an important point in her discovery of land and self. The poem is not only a simple statement of doubleness, but also an assertion of the wisdom that comes through duplicity:

Two voices
took turns using my eyes:

One had manners,
painted in watercolours,...
and expended sentiment upon the poor.

The other voice
had other knowledge:
that men sweat
always and drink often,...

One saw through my
bleared and gradually
bleaching eyes, red leaves,
the rituals of seasons and rivers

The other found a dead dog
jubilant with maggots
half-buried among the sweet peas. (*JSM*, p. 42)

Moodie is doubly perceptive, able to perceive rituals AND the facts of reality, and therefore doubly wise. Following the suggestion of

39

"two voices/... using my eyes," the poem itself is both aural and visual. The poems in *The Circle Game* or *Power Politics* are emphatically visual; they must be seen on the page. The poems in the *Journals*, however, read beautifully. Even "The Double Voice" with its balanced structure succeeds aloud as well as on the page.

The poems in "Journal III 1871-1969" return to intensely realized present experience regardless of the fact that Susanna dies in the fifth of the nine poems. Armed with the knowledge of doubleness, she reflects upon the basic duplicity of life. Thus, art that rendered the wilderness bearable and had its uses there, becomes unnecessary in the civilization it alone represented in the bush ("Later in Belleville: Career"). Or Moodie sees herself, whether in daguerrotype or garden, "pitted" and "pocked" like the moon and "eaten away by light." In "Wish: Metamorphosis to Heraldic Emblem," she delights in her duplicity. Her "shrinking body / ... is / deceptive as a cat's fur." She knows her grandchildren are uneasy, seeing in her only an old puckered woman with a cameo brooch. They cannot guess at the power and vitality of her desire:

> maybe
> I will prowl and slink
> in crystal darkness
> among the stalactite roots, with new
> formed plumage
> uncorroded
> gold and
>
> Fiery green, my fingers
> curving and scaled, my
>
> opal
> no
> eyes glowing (*JSM*, p. 49)

Although metamorphosis into feline emblem will not occur, Moodie will be resurrected, and in a form more congenial to her northern, Canadian surroundings.

Her madness, in "Visit to Toronto, with Companions," reflects nature's gradual take-over of her mind. She enters an asylum land-scape with a hill, boulders, trees, but "no houses." She refuses to leave, as she had left once before in "Departure from the Bush," because "the air / [is] about to tell [her] / all kinds of answers." Her death, in "Solipsism While Dying," seems a contradiction of nature's power. I say 'seems' because the poem is ambiguous. Atwood, herself, is not a solipsist, but Moodie would like to believe that she creates the world she inhabits. At the same time, she becomes what she is through nature: "Two fires in- / formed me" (*JSM*, p. 23). The epistemological problem raised here is only partially answered by subsequent metaphors of fire, wilderness, and resurrection. Susanna herself doubts her solipsism — "Or so I thought." And the final lines of the poem point forward to the independent existence of field, lake, Toronto.

"Thoughts from Underground" and "Alternate Thoughts from Underground" are an obvious pair. In the first, despite her determination to love this country, her mind sees double and she feels split apart. The final remark gives a touch of humour to an otherwise serious book; rapidly advancing Canadian civilization still affords "no place for an english gentleman." In "Alternate Thoughts from Underground," she has shifted her point of view. Now she identifies fully with the land. Immigrant and settler are,

> the invaders of those for whom
> shelter was wood,
> fire was terror and sacred
>
> the inheritors, the raisers
> of glib superstructures. (*JSM*, p. 57)

We ignore the challenge and the lesson of double vision. We draw circles with our "closed senses." We exclude. Now that she has become one of "the stone / voices of the land" ("Resurrection"), she presents her apocalyptic vision:

> at the last
> judgement we will all be trees (*JSM*, p. 59)

Journal III ends with something of a *tour de force* in "A Bus Along St. Clair: December." Though December is hardly the time for rebirths, Susanna re-appears as an old woman on a Toronto bus to tell us — "This is my kingdom still." As Atwood explains in the "Afterword," Moodie "has finally turned herself inside out, and has become the spirit of the land she once hated" (*JSM*, p. 64), and as the spirit of this land, she cannot be confined by "concrete slabs." Just beneath the bold surfaces of our heated buildings, our weatherproof houses and malls, is "the centre of a forest." Just above us our cities is "an unexplored / wilderness of wires." What does Moodie come back to tell us? The careful order of walls and ceilings, of wires and a "silver paradise." cannot deny the insistent reality of wilderness; the spirit of the land, an old woman whose eyes shoot "secret / hatpins," has "ways of getting through."

Much of the success of *The Journals of Susanna Moodie* lies in Atwood's skilful use of the Moodie *persona*. Although the *Journals* follow the life of the historical Mrs. Moodie and reflect certain of her attitudes, they tell us primarily about Margaret Atwood's vision of the Canadian psyche. There is a little of Susanna Moodie in most of us; we are still immigrants to Canada in the parts of this vast country that we cannot inhabit, "and in the parts unknown to us we move in fear, exiles and invaders" (*JSM*, p. 62). Furthermore, seeing in Susanna Moodie something archetypically Canadian, Atwood has mythologized her heroine, not merely in terms of the past but in the living present.

The classical counterparts to Atwood's Moodie are Persephone and the Triple Goddess, Diana, Luna, Hecate.[4] Moodie has a triple role; we can see her as young woman in Journal I, as a Mother in Journal II, and as a crone in Journal III. As a chaste Diana figure in Journal I who resists being 'broken in upon', she strives to understand her immediate experience of the land; she is governed by the moon (Luna) in Journal II where she struggles with madness and the ideal of double vision; certainly, in Journal III she is a Hecate who rules the underworld, a land of living dead. In her manifestation as goddess of the underworld, Moodie is also "a double Persephone," and as such she best embodies "the spirit of this land." She *is* duality: life and death, summer and winter, nature and culture, wilderness and civilization. Having been "in- / formed" by two fires, she speaks with a double voice, accepting "the inescapable doubleness of her own vision (*JSM*, p. 63). Through the three stages of girl, woman, crone, of moon, earth, underworld, she realizes her essential duality.

Atwood's use of myth here bears striking resemblance to James Reaney's theory of myth in *Alphabet* and in his poetry. Because classical myth informs historical Canadian subjects, Reaney insists upon incarnating myth in the local present. For Reaney "metaphor is reality" and poetry is myth plus documentary — Job lives again in the Donnellys.[5] In *The Journals of Susanna Moodie*, Atwood employs a similar method, illustrating classical myth embodied in a living reality, drawn from the facts of native tradition. She shares

Reaney's belief that "the native tradition [is] ancestral, important, and haunting."[6]

I say her method is similar to Reaney's and not the same, because by the time of *The Journals of Susanna Moodie*, Atwood gives priority to native tradition not to classical mythology. In *Double Persephone* she began with the Greek story and tried to re-incarnate it, with only partial success. In the *Journals*, she begins with history, fact or document, and gradually reveals the mythic dimensions of her subject — an exciting process.[7] In this she reminds me most forcibly of Sheila Watson whose *The Double Hook* also presents a myth of duplicity rooted in Canadian soil with a strong Hecate figure in Mrs. Potter. Speaking of her use of archetype in *The Double Hook*, Mrs. Watson has said that she does not believe in the "chronological archetypes" of Northrop Frye; "the archetype is now."[8] And so it is with Moodie — she is duality, now.

It remains to examine the style of *The Journals of Susanna Moodie*, an aspect of the work usually overlooked. By style I mean, not only the language, images, and form of the poems, but Atwood's fascinating collages. Her images are by now familiar. Mirrors are important for what they reflect or do not reflect; the land itself is a duplistic mirror. Eyes exclude; without them "everything appears." Inside / outside images are important here, as in *The Circle Game*, as Moodie struggles with her environments, natural and man-made, and the inner reality and surface appearance of herself. By the time Moodie dies, she has "turned herself inside out, and has become the spirit of the land she once hated" (*JSM*, p. 64).

Language itself becomes a metaphor; thus, Moodie is at first "a word / in a foreign language." Atwood's use of language images differs from that of F. R Scott or A. M. Klein who have both given us superb metaphors of human power through language. In "Laurentian Shield," Scott traces our civilization on this continent from "Cabin syllables, / Nouns of settlement" to "a language of life, / ... written in the full culture of occupation."[9] While allowing that nature plays some role in choosing its language, he emphasizes the creative function of man. Likewise, Klein in his "Portrait of the Poet as Landscape," claims that the poet is,

> the nth Adam taking a green inventory
> in world but scarcely uttered, naming, praising,
> the flowering fiats in the meadow, the
> syllabled fur...

For to praise
the world — he, solitary man — is breath
to him. Until it has been praised, that
part has not been.[10]

Where Scott and Klein assert human priority, Atwood compromises: there is a language here, a language of "boulders, trees, no houses." The landscape talks, has answers, that we must understand if we are to belong here. Once we have learned it we will have two voices — one with old world manners, the other with new world knowledge.

There are six collages in the *Journals*, one to preface each of its three parts, and one within each of the *Journals* which seems to illustrate a particular poem. For Journal I we have Moodie as young woman set against a landscape of trees; for Journal II she is the Mother whose safe domesticity is surrounded by a threatening blur of land and bear; for Journal III we have a crone whose face reminds one of Edvard Munch's hallucinatory paintings. Each strikes exactly the right thematic note for its companion Journal. The three collages that illustrate specific poems are more obvious if no less interesting. For example, facing "Alternate Thoughts from Underground," is a collage of Moodie's buried form curved like the land she inhabits, while above her lie the straight lines of concrete, house, window, and people.

Two qualities in general strike me about these collages. They are highly expressionistic in their disjunction, their distortion of representational reality, and in their violence. They are also, by their very nature, double. In each case, Atwood has superimposed one subject on another, one style on another. The realistic, square photograph of Moodie's kitchen stands out against the engulfing ground of land and bear which is blurred in texture and curved in line. The haunting expressionistic face of Moodie is seen over against the sharp angularity of spire and building. These collages reveal the violent duality of the Moodie/Atwood world where inner vision confronts perception of external reality — as a result the rigid order of settlement and cultured self cannot remain intact. The poems themselves, unlike the majority of Atwood's verse, strike the ear. The collages assail the eye. Even the cover, also designed by Atwood, embodies duality. Resting on its side, above a sharp black/white horizontal division and between the verticle lines of grass or trees, floats the gently curved oval framing Moodies' face — the photograph of "a mad-looking and very elderly lady."

Procedures for Underground
(1970)

Procedures for Underground polarizes experience. The dominant, and initial impression of the poems is one of violence, distortion and terror but the poems of the third section are, *relatively* speaking, more personal, peaceful and affirmatory. Because the book is in three sections, a reader is tempted to think that the poems move from tension through violence to harmony, but I can find no such straightforward development. Perhaps the most apparent explanation for the calm of the final poems is that the artist has accepted and channeled the controlling powers of art and the self — with their attendant limitations. Perhaps the terror has simply been exhausted (which is not to say that the poems themselves are tired.)

Procedures for Underground is a more diffuse and uncertain book than any of the three preceding ones. I find it the least successful, as a book, despite the achievement of individual poems because the final calm is unconvincing, incommensurate with the initial violence. To assert, "I will transform / this egg into a muscle / this bottle into an act of love" (p. 73), or to claim that the clumsiness of reality can be,

> transformed
> for this moment / always
> (because I say)
>
> the sea   the shore (*PU*, p. 79)

is somehow not enough. These are fragments of art shored against the contingency of life. Indeed, this is the central problem of *Procedures for Underground*: given the presence of terror and violence, Atwood suggests that we cope, if we cope at all, through the accoutrements of modern technology ("Cyclops" and "Three Desks Objects"), through personal relationships ("Highest Altitude"), and chiefly through imaginative structures, games, language, art.

What is the terror that Atwood explores in *Procedures*? From where does it arise? The threat and violence of life presented in so many of these poems arises from 'here' — this place and this mind. In *Survival* Atwood attempts to answer the question, "Where is Here?" and her remarks are relevant. Writing about her reading of children's literature, she points out that,

45

in comic books and things like *Alice in Wonderland* or Conan Doyle's *The Lost World*, you got rescued or you returned from the world of dangers to a cozy safe domestic one; in Seton and Roberts, because the world of dangers was *the same* as the real world, you didn't.... this was a world of frozen corpses, dead gophers, snow, dead children, and the ever-present feeling of menace, not from an enemy set over against you but from everything surrounding you. The familiar peril lurked behind every bush .... (*S*, p. 30)

Whether or not one agrees that this is a legitimate insight into Canadian literature, it certainly sheds light on "familiar perils" of theme and jarring juxtapositions of matter-of-fact detail with violent disjunct image in these poems. Survival is highly problematic when there is no safe place to retreat to, when the world of danger and nightmare is *"the same* as the real world." *Procedures for Underground* explores a reality that appears innocuous at first glance, but is violent and threatening. It is, by turns, a child's world, a world of madness and dream, and an underground.

In "Eden is a Zoo" and "Game After Supper," the perspective is that of a child. The parents exist in a child's drawing complete with yellow-spoked sun. Their garden, however, is a trap, a zoo, in which they must "perform / the same actions over and over" while the speaker, less a child than humanity capturing its first parents, regards them through a fiery "hedge of spikes." "Game After Supper" invests the homeplace with an unspecified horror and menace. The game is the familiar hide-and-go-seek:

I am hiding in the long grass
with my two dead cousins,
the membrane grown already
across their throats.

We hear crickets and our own hearts
close to our ears;
though we giggle, we are afraid.

From the shadows around
the corner of the house
a tall man is coming to find us:

He will be an uncle,
if we are lucky. (*PU*, p. 7)

Undoubtedly, much of the shock in these poems comes from the cool, innocent voice which insists that there is nothing extraordinary happening. These poems, particularly "Eden is a Zoo," recall Reaney's children in *The Red Heart*, those Katzenjammer kids who inhabit a violent world barely controlled by the comic strip and their "dear fat mother." The adult point of view in "Stories in Kinsman's Park" helps to isolate the terror in a child's world. Fairy stories of witches threatening children may seem safe in the park, but at home there is no safety: one child fears "things" that get in through windows; the other has nightmares.

In "A Dialogue," the speaker locates terror explicitly: "My sister and I share the same / place of recurring dreams" (p. 12). For the sister the place is a dark swamp; for the speaker "it is a clear day." If they inhabit two different worlds that are essentially one, then who perceives the place correctly? Does the perceiver create the place perceived? Are the speaker and her sister two or one? The poem poses these questions but answers nothing. "The Small Cabin" also examines the status of objective reality, questioning whether it is separate from the perceiving mind. Because the speaker did not see the cabin burn, "the house is still there" (p. 14) in her mind. Not until she returns to the forest and sees the emptiness, will the cabin really burn. The final questions of "The Small Cabin" probe the crippling solipsism underlying many of the poems and echo Mrs. Moodie's death-bed concern and in "Solipsism While Dying" (*JSM*, pp. 52-53):

Where did the house go?
Where do the words go
when we have said them? (*PU*, p. 15)

The question of the relationship between perception and objective reality is central to *Procedures for Underground*, as it is to each of Atwood's works. Put another way it would be: Is this place terrifying or do I simply see it that way?

"We Don't Like Reminders" persists in reminding us of the danger lurking behind every bush — in this case chrysanthemums. The poem certainly offers no answer to the perceptual conundrum. Because it is such a terse and dramatic example of the 'danger within the real' that I have been discussing, I would like to quote it in full:

47

When they are dry and rattle
in the wind, when their
petals are bloodless, then
we will get rid of them

    My self compulsively moving
    objects back from the edges of tables,
    afraid of falling
    watching the life drain out of my fingers

Danger danger danger say
the chrysanthemums like
spotlights flashing
once before they go out

    Yesterday the sun was
    too quick for me,
    it got across the sky before
    I had time to see it.

The cut chrysanthemums sit
on top of my head in a streaked
milk bottle; I hear feet,
someone clipping the grass. (*PU*, p. 22)

It is not until the third line of the fifth stanza that one realizes the
position of the speaker. She is speaking from her grave.
Underground and grave must, then, be metaphors, but the poem appears factual and conversational. It is typical of Atwood to use
metaphor in this way, subtly, without the reader realizing his own
danger until it is too late. The result is that the entire poem becomes
a metaphor for duality: what is ordinary is fantastic, what is safe is
dangerous, what is alive is dead. And we, who are associated with
the "I" of the poem, do not like to be reminded that things are not
what they seem.

A closer look at the poem reveals warnings that should prepare
us for the shock of the last stanza. The first four stanzas are completely disjunct; no logical or semantic connections can be made
between or among them. They are joined in terms of images of death
— bloodless petals, life draining from fingers, stoplights flashing
danger, a vanished sun. Although flowers, tables, and stoplights are
ordinary enough, their unexplained juxtaposition in these stanza
fragments creates uneasiness. Furthermore, the voice in the first four
stanzas is dislocated, speaking from two distinct points of view. In
stanzas one and three, it is a third person voice, cool and impersonal.
In the second and fourth stanzas, we have a first person speaker voic-

ing personal uneasiness. Following the voice we move from outside to inside, from external objects to private anxiety. Most important, perhaps, in a poem about reminders, we move temporally, from a sense of the future in stanzas one and three, to the present in two and four. The future brings death: "*when* they are dry and rattle" and "stoplights flashing / once before they go out." The speaker's anxiety arises from her helplessness to stop the movement of time as it speeds, like the sun across the sky, towards death. The disjunction, both semantic and visual (the displacement of the stanzas), conveys the terror of her helplessness, for one cannot affect something with which one has no connection.

In the fifth stanza, the two halves of the poem come together: chrysanthemums are related to speaker, object and subject meet, the present ("the cut chrysanthemums sit") waits. The tactile and visual images of the preceding stanzas give way to the more encompassing aural sense. Even the semi-colon suggests a connection absent elsewhere. However, the tension in the last stanza undercuts, for me, any sense of reassurance that might arise from connections; the crysanthemums are "cut", the sharp word overpowering the softer one, and the grass is being clipped, arranged quite apart from the speaker's volition. The "streaked / milk bottle" is especially disquieting as the violent sound of the word "streaked" contradicts its sense of blurred edges. This final stanza reminds me forcibly that nothing is certain or predictable; either the dead can speak, or the speaker is mad. The stanza is taut with questions that thrust us back into the contingency and disjunction of the poem.

"We Don't Like Reminders" introduces the metaphor of underground which, as I suggested above, embodies the idea of duplistic reality — safe/dangerous, ordinary/fantastic. In terms recalling the Persephone myth which has become a staple in Atwood's work, "Procedures for Underground" finally tells us how to live in such a world. First, the poet describes the "underland." It is a duplicate of this land, with small differences — the sun is green, "the trees and rocks are the same / as they are here, but shifted" (*PU*, p. 24). If one can descend and return safely, one can obtain wisdom and power, but, like Persephone, one must eat nothing. One's friends "will be changed and dangerous." For this experience of duality there is the price of isolation and fear, the threat of madness.

Feelings of danger and terror are most acute in part I of *Procedures for Underground*, although part II offers some startling examples as well. In part I it is primarily nature that seems threatening, but in part II we see that the city is equally ominous. "The End of the World: Weekend, Near Toronto," "For Uncle M.," "Dreams of the Animals" and "Three Desk Objects," each presents ordinary situations and then uncovers the fear lurking just below the polished surface. In part III, the poet controls fear by containing it. The implication is that we can only hold onto sanity and peace through borders and the stasis of art. I think it is this urge to contain or control chaos by surrounding it that explains the dominant style of the poems in part III and certain poems, such as "Projected Slide of an Unknown Soldier," from the previous sections.

The poems in *Procedures* are emphatically visual. A few, such as "We Don't Like Reminders," are double and self-reflexive like the poems in *The Circle Game*. Others — "Weed Seeds near a Beaver Pond," "Return Trips West" and "Fragments: Beach" — comprise a number of interacting sections. The greatest number of poems, however, are visual in a specific pictorial sense; in title, subject, structure they suggest analogies with visual art. For example, the titles of "Buffalo in Compound: Alberta" or "Younger Sister, Going Swimming" describe a subject by placing it visually. The intention is quite distinct from titles such as "For Uncle M." or "Stories in Kinsman Park" because we immediately form an image in the mind's eye of buffalo or sister.

The tension between art and life, safety and danger, order and chaos, space and time, is most dramatic in "Projected Slide of an Unknown Soldier." The soldier's cry, whether a "howl / ... of agony" or a command, is silent. The face, depersonalized and disjunct, is still, captured in the square frame of the slide and the formal balance of the poem. Moral context for this emotionally distanced image rests in chiaroscuro:

Upon the wall a face
uttered itself
in light, pushing
aside the wall's darkness; ...

The mouth was filled with darkness.
The darkness in the open mouth
uttered itself, pushing
aside the light. (*PU*, pp. 46-47)

This poem, like the Moodie collage for the third journal, recalls Edvard Munch, in this case "The Scream." Through visual metaphor and pictorial analogy, the poem presents violence and terror at the same time as it renders them bearable by distancing emotion with a tightly balanced control of word and image.

"Woman Skating" is one of the best examples of the deliberate pictorial and static quality that the poet desires. The opening lines of the poem develop the image in the title through further images of place, time, and colour. The scene is very familiar to the Canadian or northern eye, and it is controlled, visually, by the skater, "concentrating on moving / in perfect circles" (*PU*, p. 64). At this point, however, the painterly illusion is broken by a parenthetical prose interjection: in the *real* scene the poet's mother is not skating at all; the ice is not a 'group of seven' lake, but an "outdoor skating rink near the cemetary" surrounded by buildings and cars; the snow is dirty and her mother's colours are "faded." With reality neatly enclosed in parentheses, the poet returns to the artistic illusion, but it is through the juxtaposition of the two scenes that one understands the transforming and controlling power of art:

    Seeing the ice
    as what it is, water:
    seeing the months
    as they are, the years
    in sequence occurring
    underfoot, watching
    the miniature human
    figure balanced on steel
    needles (those compasses
    floated in saucers)on time
    sustained, above
    time circling: miracle (*PU*, p. 65)

Just as ice shapes water, is "time sustained," just as the skater controls space, her skate blades "compasses" and her "perfect circles" time-space miracles, so the artist captures the moment, the scene:

    Over all I place
    a glass bell (*PU*, p. 65)

Not only is this poem visual, in the sense that it must be seen, it also draws upon the visual imagery of painting and the abstract concepts of time and space to emphasize the hypostasizing power of art.

The following poem, "Younger Sister, Going Swimming," suggests that art cannot stop time or flow: "The words ripple, subside, / move outwards toward the shore." The contradiction underlying these two poems is not resolved in *Procedures*. On the one hand, the poet suggests that language itself is too flexible, a "syntax of chained pebbles." On the other hand, in the last poems she accepts, for the time being, the controlling power of the word.

Procedures for Underground is a book of tensions and contradictions. In some ways it marks a central position in Atwood's development thus far, for she seems to turn back upon herself to question the vision of freedom emerging in *The Animals in That Country* and *The Journals of Susanna Moodie*. Paradoxically, she seems to reject the authority of objective reality in order to affirm the power of the mind and the prerogative of personal perception. This position is not solipsistic, but it is intensely private. Perhaps, for the poet, it is both a glory and curse.

It is also a recognizable study of modern *angst*:

The view to the side, below,
would be, as they say, breath-

taking; if we dared to look.
We don't dare. The curved

ledge is crumbling, the melting snow
is undermining the road,

in fear everything
lives, impermanence
makes the edges of things burn (*PU*, p. 56)

Whereas in *The Circle Game* and *The Journals of Susanna Moodie* Atwood reiterated the need to open to experience, to include instead of exclude, in *Procedures for Underground*, the terror of reality, the threat of "curved" space, the impermanence of human life, demands the counter-force of the mind and will. While the power of art and of the mind to control life, is some consolation here, it is fraught with the dangers that Atwood explored in *Double Persephone* or in a poem such as "Progressive Insanities of a Pioneer." Art freezes life while the mind is finally destroyed by the effort to impose its order upon chaos. It would seem that we must lose either way — on the one hand, we cannot survive the impact of reality, on the other, we entrap ourselves in our own order, our games, our cities, our art. *Procedures for Underground* does not solve this dilemma. The final poem, resting in the order of will and art, presages continued struggle — power politics.

Chapter IV

Two Islands

There are two islands
at least, they do not exclude each other

On the first I am right,
the events run themselves through
almost without us,...

The second I know nothing about
because it has never happened; (*YAH*, p. 69)

Power Politics
(1972)

The first thing that strikes one about Atwood's fifth book of
poems, *Power Politics*, is the cover. The design is a parody of the
Tarot card for sacrifice, better known as the Hanged Man.[1] The
basic position of the figure hanging by one foot with hands behind
the back is accurate enough, but the figure is clearly female and she
hangs, not from a tree, but from the right hand of a knight, his visor
firmly closed. The image is undeniably sexual, but the subject of the
Hanged Man card, as well as Atwood's theme in *Power Politics*, is
not merely sexual politics: in the Tarot, the tremendous power of the
twelfth card is used in sacrifice of self for others; in *Power Politics*,
Atwood depicts the power that "is our environment."[2]

According to Atwood, power and power struggles pervade our
lives, not only in the public fields of politics and war, but also in the
private sphere of love and personal relationships. Unfortunately, we
do not keep public modes of behaviour separate from private; we
jostle, manoeuvre and manipulate constantly until the inner life
mimics the outer. Significantly, there are few titled poems and no
title poem in the collection; thus, Atwood preserves the general
thrust of her theme. Atwood found the book's title in the chance use
of the words, power politics, in a personal letter and a newspaper,
and this is how she sees the poems — as personal and public,
"halfway between letter and newspaper."[3]

Sexual politics, then, is only one aspect of the power struggle: the knight in shining armour needs a maiden to rescue and the maiden must pay for her "bronze rescue"; if she withdraws her belief, the idols of power collapse. Unfortunately, power and love are opposites; power takes and love gives. Even the attempt to break free from power struggles in order to love truly is tricky, for we too often use truth to gain the upper hand. Basically, power politics on the personal level follows the more obvious public forms of war and national politics; it assumes the adversary relationship of opposites. The power mentality posits winners and losers — there is no room for a third possibility, the "third thing" Atwood mentioned in the interview with Gibson (see p. 27 above). In the power game, man must conquer — other men, nature, women — and any process, or thing, that does not follow the rule will be ignored, excluded, annihilated.

While war and national politics provide important subjects, some of the most shocking and moving poems depict personal power politics, possibly because Atwood feels that power is even more destructive in the personal realm than the public. Of course, the personal poems expose a reality in our private lives that we like to pretend is not there, or at least, to hide from public view. They are frightening, depressing, violent poems jagged with aphorisms:

I love you by
sections and when you work. (*PP*, p. 9)

Please die I said
so I can write about it (*PP*, p. 10)

you aren't sick & unhappy
only alive & stuck with it. (*PP*, p. 16)

(it is no longer possible
to be both human and alive) (*PP*, p. 30)

Next time we commit
love, we ought to
choose in advance what to kill. (*PP*, p. 35)

Most alarming, perhaps, is the speaker's voice which is cold, controlled, anaesthetized. Conversely, language and metaphor are personal, colloquial and familiar. The combination of word and voice achieves two effects. On the one hand, it suggests the state of shock of the speaker or the somnabulist condition of the artist whose feelings have been cauterized. Listening to Atwood read these poems in a deliberate dead monotone emphasizes this condition. The speaker suffers from shock, like a shell-shocked soldier, not only because of a failed love affair, but also because of the failure of love in the modern world. On the other hand, this combination of word and voice transforms the poems into weapons carefully pointed at our daily acquiescence, our belief that we are powerless. Language is the poet's only weapon, and in Atwood's hands, it is powerful; language is *not* "for the weak only." It is possible to be thoroughly repelled by many of these poems, but to reject them is to miss the point. They are goads to our insensibility, prophecies of disaster, warnings of what can happen, is happening. There are some tender moments which serve as antidotes, but these are easily overlooked in the power game: moments of sadness and regret —

> You rest on the bed
> watching me watching
> you, we will never know
> each other any better
>
> than we do now (*PP*, p. 14)

or of urgent pleading —

> We need each others'
> breathing, warmth, surviving
> is the only war
> we can afford, stay
>
> walking with me,... (*PP*, p. 38)

There are three sections in *Power Politics*, each one prefaced by a terse four-line poetic bombshell that establishes the tone of the following poems.[4] There is little sense of development or progression through the three parts; things remain as bad as they began. We simply look at events from different perspectives. Nevertheless, some sense of syllogistic conclusion to the predominantly static situation exists: given the violence of part one and the obtuseness and prevarication of part two, one forgets how to live; one dies. An undeniable aspect of the horror arises, in fact, from the seemingly irrefutable logic of the syllogism form. The poems can also be grouped around two areas of experience, the private and the public, the letter and the newsreel. Many of the poems recall letters or newsreels — a point I will return to. Viewed in this way we see two main streams running through the book to a common dead end — the destructive power struggle in a love affair and the history of power in war, politics, or the conquest of nature depicted in images drawn from religion and technology.

Part I explores the devastation of sexual power politics. The prefacing poem catches one off-guard:

> you fit into me
> like a hook into an eye
>
> a fish hook
> an open eye (*PP*, p. 1)

Not only does this convey the violence of sexual conquest, it forces us to look afresh at simple domestic objects such as the hook-and-eye fastener. The juxtaposition of brutal fish hook and utter vulnerability in the open eye, emphasizes the familiar Atwood point that we must learn to see properly. This poem, then, comments upon the nature of sexual warfare and forces us to recognize it for what it is.

But both partners are guilty in this game because they create roles that they expect their opposites to play. The speaker in "They eat out" is especially obnoxious because she enjoys her superior knowledge and her power to immortalize, although she knows it is destructive:

> I raise the magic fork
> over the plate of beef fried rice
>
> and plunge it into your heart.
> There is a faint pop, a sizzle
>
> and through your own split head
> you rise up glowing; (*PP*, p. 5)

We dehumanize ourselves by perpetuating these games of hero worship — adoring female creates superman "in blue tights and a red cape" who requires adoring female to maintain the illusion. This we call love. Finally, as if to add insult to injury, the speaker shrugs off responsibility:

> As for me, I continue eating;
> I liked you better the way you were,
> but you were always ambitious.

This sense of deflation is equally effective in the untitled poem ("My beautiful wooden leader," *PP*, p. 7) that suggested the cover drawing. The speaker *knows* that the "wooden leader" is a loser, victimized by the game he plays. She knows the "floral tributes" are not love and that the lovers are trapped in lies. She is the proverbial maiden, also the fickle populace, betraying and betrayed:

My love for you is the love
of one statue for another: tensed

and static....
though you promise bronze rescues

you hold me by the left ankle
so that my head brushes the ground,
my eyes are blinded,
my hair fills with white ribbons.

There are hordes of me now, alike
and paralyzed, we follow you
scattering floral tributes
under your hooves. (*PP*, p. 7)

There is no sense here of the efficacy of ancient wisdom. The speaker, presumably female, is blind and paralyzed. The hanged man of the twelfth arcanum should symbolize the power of sacrifice on three traditional levels: archetype, man and nature. Archetypally, he is Christ, but this leader, despite the floral tributes that recall Christ's welcome to Jerusalem, does nothing constructive. As a human being he is equally ineffectual; he uses others to affirm his own failed reality. Even the sun, the natural embodiment of life-giving self-sacrifice, suggests indifference:

The sun sets, and the people all
ride off in the other direction. (*PP*, p. 7)

The scenario would be farcical if it were not a sad impasse. Part I of *Power Politics* concludes on this note of futility. "Their attitudes differ" presents a type of truce that in fact frustrates real *rapprochement*:

To understand
each other: anything
but that,... (*PP*, p. 10)

57

The three parts of this poem mirror the larger structure of the book. Common to each is the mechanization that simplifies life by killing it. Whether as spy, biologist, or coroner, we respond to life and love with clinical reason. It is perhaps some comfort that the speaker acknowledges the impasse of mutual victimization and betrayal with sadness in the final poem of the section.

The poems in part II are less violent and metaphorical than the preceding ones. For the most part, they are simple, direct descriptions or statements of hostility. The prefacing poem establishes the central conflict in political/natural terms:

> Imperialist, keep off
> the trees I said.
>
> No use: you walk backwards,
> admiring your own footprints. (*PP*, p. 15)

We treat each other the way a colonizing nation treats the land or a weaker nation.

Atwood places the blame squarely on human shoulders: "You did it / it was you who started the countdown." It is difficult to dissociate the "you" from male and the "I" from female in this poem, especially as the "I" is associated with nature, but such categories are unnecessarily limiting. It is mankind who is being addressed, who sets up the opposites, the power structures, and suffers accordingly:

> When will you learn
> the flame and the wood/flesh
> it burns are whole and the same?
>
> You attempt merely power
> you accomplish merely suffering (*PP*, p. 32)

Unlike the maiden in "My beautiful wooden leader" or the speaker in "They eat out," the speaker here withdraws support:

> I'm through, I won't make
> any more flowers for you
>
> I judge you as the trees do
> by dying (*PP*, p. 33)

This poem makes two points about the nature of power politics. The first of them is pathetically ironic. Because we divide the world into two, just as the protagonist's brother in *Surfacing* does with the leeches, we negate the underlying unity in life — the fact that "the flame and the wood/flesh" are the same. Atwood implies here that subject and object are one, that by polarizing them we *create* power and suffering. Still more important, through earlier images of countdown, machines and electrified fences, she isolates a particular context for this suffering. This is the modern technological world where Cartesian rationalism reaches its apogee in "an impervious glass tower" in which humanity seals itself off from nature.

The problems involved in the concept of the unity of all things are not resolved in *Power Politics*, but the poet does probe the failure of modern life. As a result of our Cartesian view of the world we have denied the vitality of our contexts — nature and body — until, in our pride, we no longer recognize the need for a context. One of the prime sources of anxiety in *Power Politics* is the lack of meaningful context. In "He shifts from east to west," the speaker admits,

> Because we have no history
> I construct one for you
>
> making use of what
> there is,... (*PP*, p. 26)

Assembled fragments, however, are unsatisfactory. The sense of irrelevance and contingency is overwhelming; you remain,

> suspended in the air with no more
> reason for occurring
> exactly here than this billboard,
> this highway or that cloud. (*PP*, p. 27)

In "At first I was given centuries," the problem becomes increasingly acute through the ages until today we are reduced to empty roles and public functions. We have "long forgotten the difference / between an annunciation and a parking ticket" (*PP*, p. 30). Today it "is no longer possible / to be both human and alive" (*PP*, p. 30).

The final poem in Part II, "They are hostile nations," is an eloquent plea for disarmament before destruction is final. Given the pollutions of modern life, "we should / take warning," we should relinquish our adversary positions, be careful that our gifts are not Trojan horses:

> Here there are no armies
> here there is no money
>
> It is cold and getting colder
>
> We need each others'
> breathing, warmth, surviving
> is the only war
> we can afford, stay
>
> walking with me, there is almost
> time / if we can only
> make it as far as
>
> the (possibly) last summer (*PP*, p. 38)

If we can survive this season of death, we just may be able to reach the new life of summer. But there is no room for easy optimism. "Possibly" it will be our last summer.

In any case, Part III does not open on an encouraging note. It may be "spring again," but we have lost the desire to live:

> Returning from the dead
> used to be something I did well
>
> I began asking why
> I began forgetting how (*PP*, p. 39)

This need for rebirth or resurrection echoes through much of Atwood's work, back into *The Journals of Susanna Moodie* and *Procedures for Underground* and forward into *Surfacing*. But in *Power Politics* there is no rebirth. Instead there is continued winter and death, the result of power politics in public and private life.

Death comes in many forms. In "This year I intended children," the hope for fructification, children, strawberries, "fur seeds & burrows," dies violently (murder or suicide?):

> but the entrails of dead cards
> are against me, foretell
> it will be water (*PP*, p. 41)

If these are the Tarot cards, then the card the speaker draws foretells a violent death by drowning in images associated with the Hanged Man. Whether as mother or poet, the creative force is dead:

> upside down, lifesize, hair streaming
> over the slashed throat
> and words fertilize each other
> in the cold and with bulging eyes (*PP*, p. 41)

I do not find here either the defiance of Klein's drowned poet or the beauty that transforms D. C. Scott's "Piper of Arll." Nor is there the ambivalence that allows for rebirth in the "Death by Water" section of Eliot's *The Wasteland*. Because the throat is slashed there can be no utterance, no communication. Words fertilize each other, not our thought or feelings, with the "bulging eyes" of the drowned.

Sexual love becomes assault, monstrous and murderous. The speaker in "What is it," both as woman and landscape, is raped. In "You are the sun," she realizes she has created this monster who reverses the natural order, but does not know how to stop it or why she created it in the first place. The generous gesture of assistance is no help because to help is to assume power and power is the enemy (*PP*, p. 43). The truth is corrosive even when the speaker admits her culpability for the creation of roles — "It was my fault but you helped, / you enjoyed it" (*PP*, p. 55) — the lovers remain locked in selfishness. Gifts are especially lethal. Part III closes with this reminder that we are trapped by the gifts of others, and there is no better Atwood metaphor for this kind of death than the glass paperweight:

> The death you bring me
> is curved, it is the shape
> of doorknobs, moons
> glass paperweights
>
> Inside it, snow and lethal
> flakes of gold fall endlessly
> over an ornamental scene,
> a man and woman, hands joined and running (*PP*, p. 56)

Many of the poems in *Power Politics* have the informal conversational tone of personal letters. At times these poems seem directed outwards, efforts at communication that become weapons as in

61

"You refuse to own" (*PP*, p. 30), or "You did it" (*PP*, p. 32). At other times, they seem meant as much for the speaker as for a listener; they function as a release from pain, like biting on an aching tooth. Hence, the speaker adopts a courageous pose in "You have made your escape" where "You" have disappeared leaving no forwarding address while "I" remember you, as if nothing had gone wrong, by "the bruises / on my thighs and the inside of my skull" (*PP*, p. 13). "There are better ways of doing this" seems more like a diary entry than a letter with its anatomy of private pain endured, ironically, for its public image.

A few of the poems deliberately invoke the world of newspaper and newsreel. Atwood has called "At first I was given centuries" a "newsreel" poem.[5] It might also be called a documentary as it presents images of war, from the woman's point of view, from prehistoric times, through the Crusades and both World Wars, to our present constant hostility. Time speeds up in several senses. The centuries spent waiting in caves give way to years, months, weeks, seconds. The periods of peace become shorter and shorter until there are none. All history rushes into continuous conflict obliterating, as it goes, every context and all meaningful communication. Here Atwood uses the "newsreel" analogy to accentuate the sense of a headlong rush towards death. Also, she applies the public technique of newsreel to the private domain, thus emphasizing her belief that the power politics of war destroys on both levels.

"Small Tactics" uses the more specific film technique of montage. Each of its seven sections is a separate unit, like an individual frame. Together, the sections create a jerky fragmented narrative that moves, frame by frame, like a silent movie. Individual lines are spasmodic:

Me trying to give
the impression it isn't

getting bad   at least
not yet (*PP*, p. 19)

or are elliptic, cut off:

Can't play it safe, can't play
at all any more (*PP*, p. 17)

The seven fragments tell the story of a relationship in which all forms of public communication have failed — the news media bring no news, the telephone produces "Wire silences." With terrible irony, the speaker prays for the closed insensate utility of an electric lightbulb. In the final section, she describes her revenge. After such private failure and pain, one cannot expect public acclaim or even a tombstone:

> You will have nothing
> but me and in a worse way than before,
>
> my face packed in cotton
> in a white gift box, the features
>
> dissolving and re-forming so quickly
> I seem only to flicker. (*PP*, p. 20)

In exchange for the pain of honesty or "this trap / this body," he will have the gift of a severed head with a celluloid face. The closing image completes the logic of the film analogy; modern communications, when applied to personal realities, reduce life to a meaningless blur.

In *Power Politics*, Atwood explores the nature of power, and as the cliché has it, power corrupts. Power also destroys because it insists upon one exclusive pattern of winner/loser, victor/victim. Either things are right or wrong, good or bad. Through these poems Atwood shows how power struggles colour everything we do, turning even our most sacred activities into deadly manoeuvers that, finally, destroy both sides. The modern dilemma is particularly acute because a power politics mentality armed with modern technology has annihilated all contexts but its own. Life now has no purpose; the game of power politics has, seemingly, no exit.

But is there a good power? During the C.B.C. program devoted to the collection, Atwood mentioned three zodiacal symbols of power — the Scorpion representing physical power over others, the serpent representing intellectual powers, and the eagle representing power over the self.[6] It is the third form of power that enables us to govern our own will, to choose *not* to play power politics. Until we recognize, however, exactly what we are doing, we will be powerless to change. And this is the profoundly moral purpose of these poems — to shock us with recognition. But what do we do if we accept Atwood's mirror of ourselves? What does one do with the truth? Within the context of *Power Politics*, all we *can* do is hold on like the dwarf trees and mosses "hooked into" the rock of reality: "Beyond truth, / tenacity."

You Are Happy
(1974)

It is no coincidence that the publication of Atwood's next collection of poems was followed in 1976 by the publication of her first *Selected Poems*. *You Are Happy* contains echoes of preceding works and offers, in fact, a summation of the poetic journey thus far. In many ways, it marks a plateau from which Atwood surveys the territory behind her before setting out again to continue her explorations. The new volume, *Two-Headed Poems*, offers fresh developments in voice and subject, but fundamental questions of duplicity, epistemology, and nature of the self remain.

You Are Happy repeats the violence and anger of *Power Politics*, the vicious circles of *The Circle Game* and, occasionally, the highly metaphorical hallucinatory vision of *Procedures for Underground*. The sense of self as a landscape, here an island, is very strong, as it was in *The Animals in That Country* and *The Journals of Susanna Moodie*. The central theme is the nature and function of perception which has been important throughout her work: how do we see ourselves or others? How are we seen by others? How do we learn to see freshly, to free ourselves from roles, functions, myths? What *is* perception? She returns to the use of myth, recalling *Double Persephone* and the *Journals*, but from a new point of view. The inimitable Atwood voice, of course, is pervasive — caustic, comic, satiric, ruthless, occasionally tender, and never to be taken for granted. In addition to new insights into myth, she gives us nine poems of reconciliation, harmony and hope.

There are four sections in *You Are Happy*, unlike the usual tripartite structure in Atwood's work, and this is a welcome change from the relentless syllogistic form of *Power Politics*. Because many of the poems are difficult to understand in isolation from the others, the urge to connect, to read them sequentially as one would a narrative, is strong. Atwood, I feel, wants us to make and understand the need for connections. In general, the poems present hostility in I, ironic warnings in II, choices in III, and a final wholeness in IV. But the intensely metaphoric connections are not easy to make. One experiences this problem not only between poems or sections of the book, but between sections I, II, III, and the final section. While section IV is convincing in its own right, it is less so as the outcome of the preceding parts. Perhaps the poems in "There is only one of everything" should be viewed, not so much as a conclusion or outcome, as an alternative, a possibility.

Part I is subtitled "You Are Happy." The poems present futility, withdrawal, fury, and pain. The title poem is bitterly ironic:

We walk separately
along the hill to the open
beach,...

In the ditch a deer
carcass, no head. Bird
running across the glaring
road against the low pink sun.

When you are this
cold you can think about
nothing but the cold, the images

hitting into your eyes
like needles, crystals, you are happy. (*YAH*, p. 28)

The images of separation and dissociation, particularly that of the deer carcass, capture the sense of fragmentation that characterizes so many of these poems. There is no context for this walk. These people are frozen, immobilized by the cold. In this state, happiness is a blinding mockery of life. Several of the images in this poem, the walkers, the cold, birds, the deer, recur in a later poem, "There are two islands" (*YAH*, pp. 69-70), in a more hopeful context; in this poem the lovers walk in a landscape "not frozen yet," and as if time has turned back, the deer is present only by its tracks in the mud. Implicit here is a method for reading *You Are Happy*. The poems exist sequentially, but in order to understand them we can complement a linear reading with a reflexive one, working back and forth over the poems in terms of the images. Thus, the sense of walking on a beach finds new contexts in "There are two islands" from Part III and in "Four Auguries" from Part IV.

"Chaos Poem" is an excellent example of the type of fragmented moment that causes the disorientation of Part I. We enter the poem *in medias res*, like peeping Toms or eavesdroppers listening in to a conversation of which we missed the essential beginning, for which the ending is abrupt and inconclusive. The poem expresses the enervation of the speaker: "I'm getting fat, / scenarios wipe me out / in advance and my wrists are lazy" (*YAH*, p. 12). Chaos is not simply matted cat fur and crusted plates or a disintegrated love affair.

65

Chaos equals failure. In response to failure, the speaker offers further perversions of life: "at night I can hear / death growing in me like a baby with no head" (*YAH*, p. 14). In "Digging" the injured speaker creates defences. She digs in the barnyard of the past, "the archeology of manure," searching for a *memento mori* that she can wear as an amulet:

> to ward off anything
>
> that is not a fact,
> that is not food, including
> symbols, monuments,
> forgiveness, treaties, love. (*YAH*, p. 20)

Clearly, her response to pain or failure here, is withdrawal. She will avoid risk by reducing life to the certainty of facts. She will use the richness of the dungpile *only* "to feed the melons."

"Tricks with Mirrors" shifts the tactics. Instead of aiming her anger inward in self-destructive gestures, the speaker aims at "you" (at us). This poem is a marvellous example of Atwood's deadly sense of humour. Her target? — male narcissism. "Mirrors / are the perfect lovers" because they reflect a flattering image of the self. But, like everything else, this mirror image has a price. Firstly, it is most trying to be the mirror:

> Don't assume it is passive
> or easy, this clarity
>
> with which I give you yourself.
> Consider what restraint it
>
> takes: breath withheld, no anger
> or joy disturbing the surface
>
> of the ice. (*YAH*, p. 26)

In order to be a mirror, a perfect lover, the woman must repress her own identity. She is ignored for her efforts. In addition, the man loses a chance for love and freedom. Instead of contacting another warm human being,

it will be your own
mouth you hit, firm and glassy,

your own eyes you find you
are up against closed   closed (*YAH*, p. 24)

If it is really safety in the form of icy stasis that he wants, then a
crafty mirror is the answer.

This particular mirror, however, wants to break free from the
roles that entrap them both. Predictably, faulty perception is responsible, hence, the appropriateness of the mirror symbol:

I wanted to stop this,
this life flattened against the wall,

mute and devoid of colour,
built of pure light,

this life of vision only, split
and remote, a lucid impasse (*YAH*, p. 27)

The life of mirrors is remote and split because it is merely a reflection of reality, while the "life of vision" is "a lucid impasse" because
it is exclusively visual. Here, as in other poems, Atwood describes
the limitations of sight in McLuhanesque terms. The exclusive
reliance upon the visual sense separates objects in space, splits things
off from their contexts, isolates the viewer from the thing viewed. By
simply looking *at* something we are able to keep ourselves at a distance, uninvolved. As early as "A Place: Fragments" in *The Circle
Game*, the speaker recognized the need for three-dimensionality:

An other sense tugs at us:
we have lost something,...

that informs, holds together
this confusion,...

something too huge and simple
for us to see. (*CG*, p. 76)

But in "Tricks with Mirrors," the man continues to ignore her warnings so that the speaker resorts to quiet threats. She points out that
the mirror has a frame and a back with "several nails." Nails are

sharp, like the warnings in the poem, perhaps like shards of broken glass. In case he has missed the point, she concludes:

You don't like these metaphors.
All right:

Perhaps I am not a mirror.
Perhaps I am a pool.

Think about pools. (*YAH*, p. 27.)

According to the classical myth when Narcissus fell in love with his image reflected in the fountain, he fell in and drowned.

"Songs of the Transformed" is the least successful section of *You Are Happy*. The problem is twofold. Firstly, the talking animals are obvious masks for the poet's criticism of the standard vices of greed and cruelty as, for example, in "Pig Song" and "Bull Song." A common theme is man's ruthless exploitation of a natural world for which he has little respect, but too often the poems come dangerously close to preciousness. The remarks of the fox, for example, in "Song of the Fox" are witty, but not particularly profound:

you saw me as vermin
a crook in a fur visor;
the fate you aim at me
is not light literature. (*YAH*, p. 40))

The second problem, though more serious, is potentially more challenging. Who or what is responsible for all these unfortunate transformations? In "Pig Song" the man, "a greypink vegetable with slug / eyes," addresses a specific culprit as "Madame." Is Madame Circe? Does it matter who she is? In "Bull Song," the dying victim blames himself:

A mistake, to have shut myself
in this cask skin,
four legs thrust out like posts.
I should have remained grass. (*YAH*, p. 31)

The fox, rat, and hen scarcely seem to be transformed at all — they are what they are. Why, then, are these poems called "Songs of the Transformed"?

A possible answer may be that most of these poems are meant to be beast fables. They are clearly about human life, our follies, sins, stupidity, as the head crow in "Crow Song" so succinctly points out. Furthermore, these poems seem intended to transform our perception of life by making us see things from another point of view. We are "stupid / humanist(s)" (*YAH*, p. 32), who must be reminded of the connections between animal and human, victor and victim. Perhaps Atwood is implying that the phenomenon of transformation is a basic process of life; this would seem to be the point in "Song of the Worms":

> We have been underground too long,
> we have done our work,
> we are many and one,
> we remember when we were human (*YAH*, p. 35)

If life is the great transformer, then mankind's chief sin is his interference in the process, his attempts to freeze life in a series of fixed opposites, man/animal, life/death, reality/myth. Hence, the significance of the warning in "Song of The Worms":

> Soon we will invade like weeds,
> everywhere but slowly;
> the captive plants will rebel
> with us, fences will topple,
> brick walls ripple and fall, (*YAH*, p. 35)

The world of "captive plants," fences and brick walls belongs to the rigid logic and single vision of "The Surveyors" and "Progressive Insanities of a Pioneer" (*AC*).

My reading of "Songs of the Transformed" is substantiated by "Corpse Song," the last, and best, poem in the section. "Corpse Song" is a warning:

> I bring you something
> you do not want:
>
> news of the country
> I am trapped in,
>
> news of your future:
> soon you will have no voice ...

Therefore sing now
while you have the choice

  (My body turned against me
   too soon, it was not a tragedy

  (I did not become
   a tree or a constellation

  (I became a winter coat the children
   thought they saw on the street corner

  (I became this illusion,
   this trick of ventriloquism ...

or you will drift as I do
from head to head

swollen with words you never said,
swollen with hoarded love.

I exist in two places,
       here and where you are.... (*YAH*, pp. 43-44)

The corpse voice brings us knowledge of our approaching death, and
as the owl said, "There are many ways of dying" (*YAH*, p. 36). The
corpse is dead because it denied its body — "My body turned against
me / too soon" — before it realized the importance of the flesh.
Transformation for this life-denier was appropriate. Instead of
becoming tree or star, it became a variety of illusions, most importantly, "this trick of ventriloquism."

Here, finally, is the voice we have been hearing throughout
"Songs of the Transformed" — the spokesman for the many kinds
of death embodied in the trapped animals, birds and worms, who
drifts "from head to head" swollen with unexpressed love. The fate of
the corpse leads to its warning: if we do not speak out, we too will
lose our individual voices and become merely ventriloquists; "Therefore sing now / while you have the choice." The last lines reflect the
duplistic structure of the poem as well as Atwood's view of reality.
In order to perceive the "two places," here and there, we must
cultivate "an other sense". We must accept the duality of life and the
connections that underlie that condition. Man/animal, life/death,
this country / that country are not adversaries in a power struggle, but
complementaries in a process symbolized in the sub-title of the last

section in the collection — "There is only one of everything."

Before we reach the fourth section, however, we must pass through another experience of duality in "Circe/Mud Poems." Circe's world is one of magic and transformational powers; the world of mud is soft, malleable, powerless. The poems are a sequence of Circe's monologues to the intransigent Ulysses. As the poems proceed we see the great sorceress relinquish her powers and gradually transform herself from myth to woman. Although she can de-mythologize herself, unfortunately she cannot change Ulysses who remains the ruthless epic hero to the end: "in the clutch of your story, your disease, you are helpless" (*YAH*, p. 64).

The "Circe/Mud Poems" are the most enjoyable poems in the book. Circe herself is a delight, by turns comic, cynical, haughty, vulnerable and sad. She perceives Ulysses for what he is, a spoilt adventurer, an egocentric exploiter caught up in the importance of a role that Circe describes as puerile. His power is an illusion:

> There must be more for you to do
> than permit yourself to be shoved
> by the wind from coast
> to coast to coast,..
>
> Don't you get tired of killing
> those whose deaths have been predicted
> and are therefore dead already?
>
> Don't you get tired of wanting
> to live forever?
>
> Don't you get tired of saying Onward? (*YAH*, p. 51)

But the illusory power, indicated by the passive verb, "to be shoved," does not keep him from appropriating Circe's island (Circe herself) to which he was not invited, "just lured."

When this Circe tries to transform this Ulysses, it is not to an animal, but to a real, complete man. She has already told us that "Men with the heads of eagles / no longer interest" her:

> I search instead for the others
> the ones left over,
> the ones who have escaped from these
> mythologies with barely their lives;
> they have real faces and hands,... (*YAH*, p. 47)

71

But the power fails her in the central confrontation. Her amulet, a fist strung on a chain around her neck, cannot change an impervious Ulysses:

> the fist stutters, gives up,
> you are not visible
>
> You unbuckle the fingers of the fist,
> you order me to trust you. (*YAH*, p. 57)

As the poet announced in *Power Politics* (p. 31), language "is for the weak only"; therefore, the mutterings and stutterings of Circe's "fist" are useless.

Trusting or loving this man leaves Circe vulnerable and powerless. The most impressive "poem" following this capitulation is about the mud woman. Actually, it is not a poem but prose — relatively speaking, it is shapeless like the lady herself. Prose, again like the lady, is utilitarian. This little story of the convenient sex object who presents no problems for her lovers has, of course, a moral: now that Circe has relinquished her traditional female powers she finds herself expected to be nothing more than a receptacle for his life; "is this what you would like me to be, this mud woman? Is this what I would like to be? It would be so simple" (*YAH*, p. 61). As the title "Circe/Mud Poems" suggests, the crystallizing powers of Circe and the malleability of mud are extreme opposites. Are these Circe's exclusive choices?

The possibilities inherent in Circe's transformation from myth to woman are not realized because she refuses to become a passive object who can do nothing

> but accept, accept, accept.
> I'm not the sea, I'm not pure blue,
> I don't have to take
>
> anything you throw into me. (*YAH*, p. 63)

In refusing passivity she responds, like the speaker in *The Circle Game* or *Power Politics*, by withdrawing:

> I close myself over, deaf as an eye,
> deaf as a wound, which listens

to nothing but its own pain:
Get out of here.
Get out of here. (*YAH*, p. 63)

With the chance to open out into a life free of the restrictions and stereotyping of myth lost, Circe withdraws into self-absorbed pain. She becomes angry and spiteful, breeds fresh monsters, reminds him of Penelope's manoeuvres, prophecies disaster, and finally freezes him out:

Is it too cold for you?
This is what you requested,
this ice .... (*YAH*, p. 67)

In the penultimate prose-poem, a de-mythologized Circe again speaks with the tenderness and bewilderment of her humanity. Ulysses has refused to leave his prescribed role in the story, and "It's the story that counts." According to the story, Ulysses will abandon her on her island, trapped in her traditional role of sorceress, a role in which she can no longer believe:

In the story the boat disappears one day over the horizon, just disappears, and it doesn't say what happens then. On the island that is. It's the animals I'm afraid of, they weren't part of the bargain, in fact you didn't mention them, they may transform themselves back into men. Am I really immortal, does the sun care, when you leave will you give me back the words? Don't evade, don't pretend you won't leave after all: you leave in the story and the story is ruthless. (*YAH*, p. 68)

The remarkable aspect of this passage is the point of view. Throughout we have listened to the story of Ulysses' visit to the island of Aeaea from Circe's point of view. This is the story *not* told in the *Odyssey*. Her questions indicate that Circe still lives inside a story that has not been told. Although Circe may fail to transform her Ulysses from myth to man, her failure is not total; she does succeed in revealing the real face behind the enchantress mask as both more and less than the myth. Above all, she tells her own fascinating story. The fact that it is unfinished is perhaps not as bad as it may, at first glance, seem.

"Circe/Mud Poems" is contained by a prefacing and concluding poem. The first serves to describe Circe's island of power, to establish the importance of words (and, therefore, of the subsequent story), and to introduce us to the following poems of discovery:

> *You move within range of my words*
> *you land on the dry shore*
>
> *You find what there is. (YAH, p. 46)*

The concluding poem is more important. The two islands are Circe and Ulysses and their two stories. Ulysses' story is closed, static, a story of power politics which she knows by rote:

> *On the first I am right,*
> *the events run themselves through*
> *almost without us,...*
>
> *I am right, it starts again,*
> *jerkier this time and faster,...*
>
> *I could recite it backwards. (YAH, p. 69)*

But Circe's story is unknown and open-ended,

> *because it has never happened;*
>
> *this land is not finished,*
> *this body is not reversible. (YAH, p. 69)*

Not only are these "two islands" two different stories, they are also two different ways of perceiving life. With the first, one sees a closed world repeating itself meaninglessly. The inhabitants are fixed in stock adversary responses. With the second, one experiences the intense reality of a felt present: "The wet flakes / falling onto our skin and melting." Life is open-ended and fresh experience is possible.

The poems in "There is only one of Everything" are affirmations of wholeness, celebrations of the uniqueness of life. They are denials, if only in the moment, of splits, aggressive opposites and power politics. All but three of the nine poems have three or more parts instead of the customary double form. Those that do involve a double structure develop forward instead of mirroring or establishing opposites. "Late August" is a good example. The opening emphasizes time: "This is the plum season," is repeated and further par-

74

ticularized in the second phase of the poem — "Now it is the crickets."

The first poem of the sequence is a prayer that recalls the dilemma of the ventriloquist in "Corpse Song." In our obsession with logic and reason, we have abandoned and abused our bodies "which were loyal most of the time." Now we must pray for forgiveness:

> O body, descend
> from the wall where I have nailed you
> like a flayed skin or war trophy
>
> Let me inhabit you, have compassion on me
> once more, give me this day. (*YAH*, p. 73)

These words, deliberately echoing the Lord's Prayer and the scene of the crucifixion, are intended not for a rational paternalistic God, but for the sacred habitation of the living self. The need to reunify head and body, reflected in the disembodied voice of the poem, is much the same as that felt by the protagonist in *Surfacing*.

In "Is/Not" there is a simplicity and clarity that is utterly convincing. Love is not a game or an illness, but a journey without predictions. Breaking free, however, is difficult, as we see in "Four Evasions" where the speaker is unable to say anything. It is easier to withdraw. "Head against White" celebrates the living moment of time rescued from the constricting bounds of space:

> To move beyond the mirror's edge, discard
> these scars, medals, to pronounce
>
> your own flesh.   Now
>
>   to be this
> man on fire, hands open and held
> out, not empty, giving
>
> time / From these hardened
> hours, these veteran
> faces, burials
>
> to rise up living (*YAH*, p. 91)

To renounce the need for crafty mirrors is to accept the reality of flesh, to accept the truth that "the flame and the wood / flesh / it burns are whole and the same" (*PP*, p. 32). These dramatic images of man on fire and flame/flesh underscore the organic, not the mystical, unity of life. The title poem "There is only one of everything" repeats in several ways the uniqueness of living things, more especially the uniquely living moment in which the speaker can say, "I want this. I want / this."

The final poem of *You Are Happy* is one of Atwood's very best. "Book of Ancestors" opens with a description of Aztec sacrifice, the tearing of the heart from a living victim as an offering to the gods of Mexico. The scene exists within "the painted border" of the carvings on a pyramid. History offers us a variety of these rituals, these prescribed steps in a dance of death meant to propitiate the "static demands" of our gods. But the poet denies this approach to life. The self is not a sacrificial object with a pre-determined role in a metaphysical system. For Atwood, the "self is a place in which things happen."[7] The self is here and now:

> History
> is over, we take place
> in a season, an undivided
> space, no necessities
>
> hold us closed, distort
> us. (*YAH*, p. 95)

Because they are not confined by set roles in a static space or "painted borders", these lovers are freer than any others in Atwood's world. The third part of the poem expands the image of the Aztec sacrifice:

> On the floor your body curves
> like that: the ancient pose, neck slackened, arms
> thrown above the head, vital
> throat and belly lying
> undefended (*YAH*, p. 96)

But the importance of this traditional pose is its ritualistic irrelevance; "this is not an alter, they are not / acting or watching." Still extending the Aztec metaphor, Atwood presents the final paradox of the individual open and vulnerable, yet alive and whole. If we can perceive life as the process of becoming instead of the state of being, we will be able to embrace the risk of living:

76

You are intact, you turn
towards me, your eyes opening, the eyes
intricate and easily bruised, you open

yourself to me gently, what
they tried, we
tried but could never do
before . without blood, the killed
heart . to take
that risk, to offer life and remain

alive, open yourself like this and become whole (*YAH*, p. 96)

As I said earlier, the last poems, especially "Book of Ancestors,"
are moving affirmations of tenderness, love, and communication.
They provide an element of hope in a collection of poems
dominated by antagonisms, frustrations, and withdrawals. In
themselves they are convincing. The sensuous language —
"luminous," "burns," "curves" — and the longer lines that inform
"Book of Ancestors," for example, are in striking contrast to the
style and form of much of the earlier poetry. But I have reservations.
"Book of Ancestors" or "There is only one of everything" or, in
fact, any of the other nine poems in this fourth part of *You Are Happy* is more an instruction or description than an enactment. In
"Book of Ancestors" it is the object seen, the lover, who opens to life
and becomes whole. There is also a need for the transformation of
the speaker from observer to celebrant. One way that Atwood strives
to convey this sense of full participation is through the language, but
it is not quite enough. The speaker still seems trapped behind her
eyes and voice, the artist, by her art.

The power of art to freeze life was a theme in Atwood's earliest
poems, and the plight of the girl with the gorgon touch is constantly
relevant through each of the main books of poetry. At the end of
Procedures for Underground, the artist sought refuge from the
"green vision" of life as process in the static forms of art, while at the
same time realizing the psychological and sociological limitations of
pre-determining structures. This is, I feel, a fundamental dilemma that
Atwood has not yet resolved: by its very nature the printed word on
the page, the poem, stops life. How can a writer capture the proces-
ses of life in his art? Malcolm Lowry attempted it and the effort
helped to destroy him. Margaret Laurence grapples with the same
problem in *The Diviners* with limited success. Al Purdy, who firmly
believes in the necessary flux of life, offers us his "Postscript"

poems:

> I say the stanza ends
> but it never does
> there being something continual,
> apart from the blaze of man, in a woman —[8]

As Atwood knows only too well, art is the final trap. Some further sense of dynamic enactment on the part of the speaker in the poem is needed to create the illusion of complete freedom. Although Atwood does not let her Muse have the final word in *You Are Happy*, it is with the ironic "Siren Song" that I would like to end. The Siren, part bird part woman, is a cursed Muse. She asks for freedom from her "bird suit" and mythical role, but her song is the final deception:

> This song
>
> is a cry for help: Help me!
> Only you, only you can,
> you are unique
>
> at last. Alas
> it is a boring song
> but it works every time. (*YAH*, p. 39)

Chapter V

Versions of Reality

Jeannie isn't real in the same way that I am real. But by now, and I mean your time, both of us will have the same degree of reality, we will be equal: wraiths, echoes, reverberations in your own brain.

(Giving birth," *DG*, p. 242)

The price of this version of reality was testing the other one.

(*EW*, p. 271)

In an effort to distinguish between creating a poem and a novel, Atwood has remarked:

You can talk about it, but not very successfully. A poem is something you hear, and the primary focus of interest is words. A novel is something you see, and the primary focus of interest is people.[1]

Distinctions between poetry and prose can become gratuitous, nowhere more so than with Margaret Atwood. Her poems need to be seen on the page as well as heard, while the power of language in her best prose is fully realized when read aloud. Indeed, I am most struck with what George Woodcock calls the "capillary links between her poetry, her fiction (and) her criticism."[2]

Despite the larger structure of narrative, her stories and novels resemble her poems not only in theme and symbol, but in tone, point of view and voice. As we have seen, many of the poems have a duplistic structure. A comparable sense of counter-weighted settings and the use of doubled or split characters are pervasive in the fiction as well. Atwood further neutralizes the distinction between prose and poetry by frequently writing poem sequences (as well as prose poems), thereby capturing the element of continuity expected in fiction.

On the basis of the stories and the three novels about to be considered, some generalizations can be made, however, about the type of fiction Atwood writes. The people in her fictional world are less the three-dimensional realistic characters of the tradional English novel than the types associated with romance. To some extent, this is a function of point of view, for each of the novels has a first person narrator tightly enclosed within a limited perspective. Quite naturally, then, perception of others will be one-sided. But even the narrators remain aloof from the reader and this sense of two-dimensionality results in large part from the cool, acerbic nature of the narrative itself. Atwood's stories, and even more so her novels, are highly plotted, often fantastic, her intention being to focus our attention upon the significance of event and pattern.

The importance of plot, together with the emphasis placed on symbol, is consistent with Atwood's view of literature in general, of language and her view of the self. A novel is not intended to simply reflect the objective world, but to offer us a mirror in which we may detect the shapes and patterns of our experience. Language itself is dangerous and deceptive; hence, the constant stretching and probing of words in the fiction (as in the poetry) until one senses that nothing can be assumed or taken for granted. Finally, Atwood's contention that the self is a place, not an ego, a view to which I return in subsequent discussion, rules out the portrayal of character in the Jamesian or Faulknerian sense; nowhere yet has Atwood given us a rounded personality, a firm sense of the self, such as I find in Margaret Laurence's Morag Gunn. Atwood's fiction is written in what I call a mixed style combining realist and romance elements. It is a style well suited to the exploration of the contingency of life, the nature of language, and the duplicity of human perception.

Dancing Girls
(1977)

Dancing Girls is a selection of representative stories which Atwood has written over thirteen years.[3] All but three of the fourteen stories have been published before; the earliest "The War in the Bathroom" appeared in James Reaney's *Alphabet* in 1964. "Training," "Dancing Girls" and "Giving Birth" are new. In general, the stories are of mixed quality, but I feel that none of them places Atwood in the first ranks of modern short-story writers like Bernard Malamud, Doris Lessing, or closer to home, Sinclair Ross,

Alice Munro, and Clark Blaise.

The stories lack variety as individual pieces while, at the same time, they do not cohere as a collection or a unit in the way that several other collections by Canadian writers do.[4] One characteristic which they have in common is the disturbing, inconclusive ending. While this is effective, especially in "The War in the Bathroom" and "The Grave of the Famous Poet," so many of the stories end in uncertainty that the sense of being left dangling becomes exasperating. This type of conclusion mars otherwise interesting stories such as "Polarities," "A Travel Piece," or "Training" — something of urgent significance, I feel, almost shines through only to be finally obscured; the irony fails.

A second quality that each story shares is the confessional/autobiographical focus, not necessarily of Atwood herself, but on the part of her fictional characters. They are, for the most part, stories of the self, involving crises of perception and identity either within the individual psyche ("The War in the Bathrooom," "When It Happens," "Giving Birth") or arising from encounters between men and women ("Polarities," "The Grave of the Famous Poet," "Hair Jewellery," "The Resplendent Quetzal"). These problems of identity and perception are recurrent, central themes in Atwood's work, and while they have been treated masterfully in short story form — Lessing's "Our Friend Judith" for example — Atwood has greater success with these themes in her poems or in the longer novel form.

Since it hardly seems necessary, nor is there space, to discuss all eleven stories, I have decided to look at Atwood's handling of the short story form and her themes in two of the more successful stories, "The War in the Bathroom" and "Rape Fantasies," as well as in each of the new stories.

"The War in the Bathroom" is a small *tour de force* in which the reader is uncertain, almost from the outset, about who is speaking. The story is written in the first person present and the tone is that of personal, direct address to the reader. The heroine of the story, however, is referred to throughout as "she," and "I" is clearly telling us about "she's" move from one flat to another followed by the mundane events of one week in the new place, presented under daily headings from "Monday" to "Sunday." At first, "I" seems to be separate from "she": "I have told her never to accept help from strangers" (p. 9). But this illusion in narrative convention soon slips — not only does "I" share "she's" bed, advise her on clothing, food, and manners, but "I" also accompanies "she" to the bathroom. It is "I" who wins the war over morning rights to the bathroom by convincing "she" to usurp the favoured time of an elderly fellow-tenant.

Who is "I"? None other than "she," of course; we are once again face to face with the double voice of the self:

> Later in the afternoon I told her that she must take a bath. She would like to have avoided it because the bathroom tends to be chilly, but I keep telling her that cleanliness and good health necessarily go together. She locked the door and I had her kneel beside the bathtub so that I could inspect it thoroughly. I found a small hair, and some lint around the drain. (*DG*, p. 14)

Perhaps "I" is "she's" conscience — "I" reads the bible — or her ego, or that other self with whom the lonely often talk. In any case, "I" is stern and decisive. "I" manages "she," and the narrative, emphatically throughout, but not without a certain *panache*. The story is a marvellously sustained unit, amusing and thought-provoking where the longer, heavier stories such as "Polarities" tend to become over-burdened both thematically and symbolically.

"Rape Fantasies" is one of Atwood's most consistently humorous pieces. Again, as in "The War in the Bathroom" or in scenes from *The Edible Woman*, Atwood offers moving, indeed profound, insights into human nature and the problems of human relationships, without over-burdening the story form. The most significant aspect of the story is the gradual revelation of the personality of the first person speaker as tough and sardonic, yet lonely and vulnerable. The story is set in a cocktail lounge where the narrator is discussing her office friends' interest in rape fantasies with a new male acquaintance. As she talks, she slowly drops her caustic tone to relate her own rape fantasies and, through these, much of her philosophy of life.

Each of her rape fantasies is both ludicrous and touchingly human. In one her would-be assailant helps her empty her purse and open a plastic lemon only to have her squirt it in his eye. In another, he suffers from acne so she sends him to her dermatologist, while in another they both have terrible colds:

> So I ask him why doesn't he let me fix him a Neo-Citran and scotch, that's what I always take, you still have the cold but you don't feel it, so I do and we end up watching the Late Show together. I mean, they aren't all sex maniacs, the rest of the

time they must lead a normal life. I figure they enjoy watching the Late Show just like anybody else. (*DG*, p. 107)

Most importantly, as the narrator herself realizes, her rape fantasies contain "a lot of conversation." She hopes that the rapist will be unable to rape someone with whom he has just had a long conversation, someone who is also human. Seen in this light, the end of the monologue is splendid in its subtle irony. The narrator, one remembers, is explaining her views in a long conversation with a stranger she has picked up in a bar and, as the statistics show, the rapist is "often someone you do know, at least a little bit" (p. 110).

Of the three previously unpublished stories, "Training" is the least successful. The young hero, Rob, the son of a surgeon, is being groomed for medical school via a summer job as counsellor in a crippled children's camp. He is, as his father would say, in training for "it," for the harsh realities of life and failure. Rob already feels himself to be a failure as a baseball player and potential doctor. Out of his heightened sensitivity and sense of inadequacy, he forms a special attachment for a crippled child, believing he sees in her alert mind trapped in a crippled body some of the frustration he feels within himself. His identification with these children is deep: "They danced like comic robots. They danced like him" (*DG*, p. 202). The story fails, however, because it is diffuse; Atwood attempts to draw too much into the frail structure of the central situation — the friendship between Rob and the child. This relationship is inadequately drawn, as is the motivation for Rob's own frustration. The domineering presence of Rob's father and successful brothers is never "shown."

"Dancing Girls," which also explores the relationship of the self to the world, is more convincing because more sharply focussed in the theme of reality versus fantasy. Atwood develops her theme through the use of parallel contexts: the solid reality of Mrs. Nolan's boardinghouse and "the dirty snow, the endless rain, the grunting cars" (*DG*, pp. 230-231) of the city gradually overwhelm the protagonist's fantasies of foreign students in exotic native costumes as well as her dreams of green spaces and flowing water. This use of parallel or double contexts, so appropriate a form for the exploration of fantasy and reality, recalls the duplistic structure of many Atwood poems.

Ann, a Canadian studying urban planning in the United States, stays in an ugly room in a cheap boardinghouse, owned by the indomitable Mrs. Nolan, but also occupied by mysterious Chinese mathematicians and an exotic tattooed Arab. In her own "native costume" of plain wool sweaters and skirts, Ann is *not* exotic. She dreams, however, of re-designing cities — "Toronto would do for a start" (*DG*, p. 227) — into pastoral paradises. The dancing girls of the title precipitate the overthrow of Ann's urban planning dreams and the "Arabian Nights" glamour of the foreign students.

One night the silent Arab throws a wild party with three "dancing girls." Because she is unwilling to become involved, Ann locks herself in her room while Mrs. Nolan handles the situation by calling the police and chasing the men from her house. Consequently, Ann does not see "the dancing girls" who "were probably just some whores from Scollay Square" (*DG*, p. 235), and does not have to relinquish entirely her image of an exotic event. She does, however, realize that her "green, perfect space of the future" has been "cancelled in advance" (*DG*, p. 236). The story closes as Ann indulges herself "one last time" in her urban fantasy:

> The fence was gone now, and the green stretched out endlessly, fields and trees and flowing water, ... The man from next door was there, in his native costume, and the mathematicians, they were all in their native costumes. Beside the stream a man was playing the flute; and around him, in long flowered robes and mauve scuffies, their auburn hair floating around their healthy pink faces, smiling their Dutch smiles, the dancing girls were sedately dancing. (*DG*, p. 236)

This time the image of a re-designed pastoral city draws together the various fantasies of the story as if in one final effort to fend off the real world of Mrs. Nolan.

There is a problem that hovers over "Dancing Girls," however, much the same problem that vitiates "Training": what motivates Ann's fantasies? Why is she drawn to the illusory exoticism of foreign students or pastoral visions of modern cities? It is easy to sympathize with her naive desire to replace the ugly sordidness of modern cities with open, green spaces. The sense of claustrophobia arising from cramped spaces (here, the boardinghouse room), closed circles, or rigid squares is a constant Atwood preoccupation for which Ann is an exponent. Perhaps the attraction of the students with their "native costumes" can only be explained in terms of Ann's insecure sense of her own identity. As a Canadian in the United States she is not perceived as distinct, let alone foreign; she does not have a "native costume" (*DG*, p. 231).

"Giving Birth" is by far the most interesting and challenging story in the collection. It is, I feel, of a quality and importance equal to Atwood's finest poems. Furthermore, it is something of a personal statement on the nature of the creative process for which the birth of a child is an obvious metaphor. What is being born, however, is more than, or *other* than, a baby; it is a story, and an aspect of the self. The success of this story depends in part upon the fact that the birth is both metaphor and event. Also of importance, and handled with equal skill, is the narrative voice. These two elements of the narrative are inextricably woven together.

Approximately two thirds of the way through "Giving Birth," the first person narrator asks herself why she must try to describe "events of the body" such as childbirth: "why should the mind distress itself trying to find a language for them?" (*DG*, p. 249) The story is the answer. The narrator begins by questioning the language we use to describe life. Words such as "giving" and "delivering" are troublesome and inadequate because they imply an end-product, an object, whereas birth like death is an event, not a thing. In order to overcome the limitations of language, in order to understand the significance of event, the narrator must, paradoxically, use language to write about the event. Thus, the narrator/writer creates her protagonist "Jeannie," named after the light-brown haired Jeannie of the song.

Atwood goes to considerable effort to distinguish between the "I" of the story and "Jeannie":

> (By this time you may be thinking that I've invented Jeannie in order to distance myself from these experiences. Nothing could be further from the truth. I am, in fact, trying to bring myself closer to something that time has already made distant. As for Jeannie, my intention is simple: I am bringing her back to life.)
> (*DG*, p. 243)

By "bringing [Jeannie] back to life" in fiction, the narrator can attempt to recapture the significance of an event for the self. The story is the writer's way of 'bringing something back' from her experience so that she will not forget entirely "what it was like" (*DG*, p. 252). Therefore, towards the end of the story, the narrator, who is still troubled by the words "giving birth" can realize that,

> (It was to me, after all, that birth was given,
> Jeannie gave it, I am the result.) (*DG*, p. 253)

The birth has been given to the narrator because it is an event that has become a part of her, that has changed her. Because the narrator is a writer, however, the reality of this event takes its final shape in language, in a story.

With the last lines of the story Atwood pinpoints the relationship between narrator/Jeannie/reader, and the nature of experience. Atwood has said that for her "the self is a place in which things happen."[5] Birth has happened to Jeannie, in the story, and through Jeannie to the narrator. The story has happened to us; it is the event we experience. Just as Jeannie's hair darkens and she "is replaced, gradually, by someone else" (*DG*, p. 254), so the narrator has changed. Atwood is asking us to reconsider the relationship between experience and the self. She is attempting, through language, to grasp the meaning of event and the significance of a universal human event for the individual self. Life, like birth and death, is a process, not a static thing or object. The self, Atwood claims, is not a hard fixed kernel, an ego, but a place where events happen, a place that is changed by events. In a sense, then, we the readers are changed by "Giving Birth."

As noted earlier, the baby in the story is more than a metaphor for the creative process; the chief protagonist does have a baby. But the story is never tiresomely gynecological in the way that Audrey Thomas' "If One Green Bottle..." finally is. Through Jeannie and her other self, the woman with "the haggard face, the bloated torso, the kerchief holding back the too sparse hair" (*DG*, p. 254), Atwood portrays the very real sense of terror and estrangment from the self that a person can feel when facing an unknown ordeal. The woman who shadows Jeannie is not "really there," but she is the embodiment both of fear and of the self's unwillingness to be absorbed by event. Jeannie and her other self, then, are the counter-weights in "Giving Birth." By writing the story, the narrator is able to absorb event into the self rather than be overwhelmed by it. Through language, 'the mind's distress,' meaning is born.

The Edible Woman
(1969)

The Edible Woman is Margaret Atwood's first published novel. Although it is, in certain ways, clearly a *first* novel, it does both entertain and present serious problems of personal identity and contemporary life. Characteristic of Atwood's narratives, *The Edi-*

ble Woman is written in a mixed style; it uses the conventions of realism and romance. This mixed style is both a delight and a difficulty in the novel as it can also be in the more problematic vision of *Surfacing*. In *Lady Oracle*, the mixture of realist and Gothic romance conventions is perhaps more acceptable because that novel is fundamentally about art, in a way that *The Edible Woman* and *Surfacing* are not.

Until the gradual takeover of fantastic event and importunate symbol, *The Edible Woman* is a simple enough story. The heroine, Marion McAlpin, recent possessor of a B.A., works for a market research company, Seymour Surveys, in Toronto. She is an average young woman with a small circle of friends and a lawyer boyfriend, Peter Wolander, who is "ordinariness raised to perfection."[6] This assessment of Peter is made by Marion's roommate Ainsley who is a touch less ordinary than Marion in that she is intent upon motherhood but determined not to marry. The plot turns upon Marion's agreement to marry Peter and her subsequent decision to escape from his cannibalistic (as she perceives them) clutches. On the periphery of this sequence of events are the contrasting (and complementary) lives of the voracious Ainsley and Marion's other female friend, Clara, who is expecting her third baby. On the outer circle of these lives hover the three office virgins who hunt with less success than Marion, Ainsley, or Clara, as well as three English graduate students, one of whom, Duncan, will nicely complicate the plot.

The story, presented in three stages, is told by Marion herself, even when she speaks in the third person. It is a witty, sarcastic, urbane anti-comedy which does not offer the traditional comic reaffirmation of the social order. Marion McAlpin provides amusing but devastating vignettes of office life, courtship, Motherhood, graduate school and, as the title implies, our consumer society. Her humour is brittle and often double-edged. For example, she concludes a love-making scene in Peter's bathtub with the following observations:

> He bit my shoulder, and I recognized this as a signal for irresponsible gaiety: Peter doesn't usually bite.
> I bit his shoulder in return, then, making sure the shower lever was still up, I reached out my right foot — I have agile feet — and turned on the COLD tap. (*EW*, p. 63)

Before too long her "agile feet" will take her out of his life, but not before he feels the shock of the lady-shaped cake. The mutual nibbling contributes a further suggestive touch to the central metaphor of eating. Indeed, Marion who loves to eat at the beginning of the novel and gradually becomes incapable of eating the more she identifies with the things eaten, constantly thinks in anthropophagic terms. It should come as no surprise that she will respond to Peter's perceived threat by making him a substitute for herself, a cake-lady, that he can eat.

In order to understand the purpose of the novel, one must assess the reliability of Marion's narrative, for the story is presented entirely through her eyes. The first and very brief third sections of the book are told in the first person singular, past tense. The long second section which recounts Marion's gradual refusal to eat and her flight from Peter, is presented in a third person past voice that is, in fact, Marion's. The narrator is entirely frank with us about this apparent aberration; she observes, in part three, that the problems of others no longer interest her: "Now that I was thinking of myself in the first person singular again I found my own situation much more interesting than his" (*EW*, p. 278). The split voice, now first person, now third, conveys Marion's sense of self-alienation. The difficulty that arises from Atwood's choice of narrative voice, however, is that neither the reader nor Marion is sure of the external cause for Marion's alienation. Because she is so encapsulated within her own point of view, Marion does not locate or understand the motivation for her behaviour. Her return to herself, signified by the resumption of first person in part three of the novel, must signify nothing more than a return to her previous normalcy as a consumer and predator.

The use of the past tense throughout underlines the fact that she is looking back upon the Labour Day weekend of part I and the ensuing months, and reflecting upon their significance. But what has she learned? Surely not that cannibalism, in any of its forms, is acceptable because 'normal'. It seems to me that Marion, like Swift's Gulliver, learns very little; her point of view is narrow if not false. We are the ones who learn — that the function of life is to eat, to destroy or be destroyed, that Marion McAlpin has a narrow escape but is, finally, one of the survivors: she can eat. We may react as we please. We can even say that Marion over-reacts, or as Duncan suggests, completely misreads the situation.

A further obstacle to understanding the significance of shift in narrative voice in *The Edible Woman* is the use of a first person *present* voice in chapter twelve, the brief final chapter of part I. This is the only point in the novel where the present tense is used, and the effect is curious. By the end of the preceding chapter Marion has agreed to marry Peter, the Labour Day weekend which was about to commence as the book opened is nearly over, and she has just returned from the laundromat where she has seen Duncan for the second time and unaccountably kissed him. Then — "So here I am":

> I'm sitting on my bed in my room with the door shut and the window open. It's Labour Day, a fine cool sunny day like yesterday....
> Friday seems a long time ago, so much has happened since then, but now I've gone over it all in my mind I see that my actions were really more sensible than I thought at the time.
> (*EW*, p. 101)

Thus, this brief chapter reflects back upon the entire first part of the novel; it is from this point in time that the events of Friday, Saturday, and Sunday have been narrated. Marion is trying to understand her behaviour — her tears in the bar, her retreat beneath Len's bed, her flight from Peter culminating in her acceptance of his marriage proposal. The reader also expects some explanation, some clue, from this present voice, for surely there is wisdom in hindsight. But Marion decides that she has been consistent with her "true personality"; she wanted Peter to propose and she set out to capture him.

This explanation only confuses the issue. If her "true personality" and her subconscious endorse her decision to marry, why does the narrative shift into an alienated third person past in part II and back to a first person past in part III? Furthermore, how does the present voice in this chapter connect, temporally, with the remaining two parts of the book where events develop chronologically over the next few months? Why has Atwood used a first person present voice at all here?

Possibly Marion has become "unstuck in time" like Vonnegut's Billy Pilgrim. Whether or not she was in full control of her actions during the weekend, she certainly does not appear to be so over the next months, and it is at this point, in the present, that her inertia takes over:

> In a minute I'll get off the bed and walk through the pool of sunshine on the floor. I can't let my whole afternoon dribble away, relaxing though it is to sit in this quiet room gazing up at

the empty ceiling with my back against the cool wall, dangling my feet over the edge of the bed. It's almost like being on a rubber raft, drifting, looking up into a clear sky.

I must get organized. I have a lot to do. (*EW*, p. 103)

From here on Marion has lost her grip on time. Not only is she an object (as she sees it) that is acted upon, she is also being swept along by the flow of the events, 'drifting on a rubber raft,' unable to affect the course of her life. This idea of drifting recurs in part II. Sitting in the office she feels "time eddying and curling almost visibly around her feet" as it carries her towards her wedding day: "She was floating, letting the current hold her up" (*EW*, p. 115). Later the same day she "drifted out of the office and down the hall and let herself be floated down in the decompression chamber of the elevator" (*EW*, p. 117). Shortly before the wedding day, we are told how she has existed over the past months:

The long time she had been moving through ... had been merely a period of waiting, drifting with the current, an endurance of time marked by no real event; waiting for an event in the future that had been determined by an event in the past; whereas when she was with Duncan she was caught in an eddy of present time: they had virtually no past and certainly no future. (*EW*, p. 184)

Neither alternative seems positive — to be drifting with Peter or to be caught in a disjunct present with Duncan.

Certainly Atwood intends her use of voice to reflect Marion's splitting or dissociation of self and her return to a unified perception of herself. The first person past voice, then, embodies a unified Marion, if not a Marion who has learned a great deal. She has at least, as Duncan says, come "back to so-called reality" (*EW*, p. 281). The section of third person narrative is quite consistent with this purpose. Chapter twelve, though intriguing, is less successful both formally and thematically. It disrupts the temporal consistency of the narrative and confuses the irony of the story.

In a discussion of style with Linda Sandler, Atwood emphasized the fact that she does not write satire but "realism verging on caricature":

I try to select characters who are outgrowths of their society. But my writing is closer to caricature than to satire — distortion rather than scathing attack — and as I say, it's largely realism. The market research scenes in *Edible Woman* are an example of realism verging on caricature, they are very slightly exaggerated...[7]

To describe Atwood's fiction as "largely realism," however, is misleading, especially for *The Edible Woman* and *Lady Oracle*. Not only are certain scenes and characters in these novels slightly exaggerated, they are extravagant, and primarily symbolic. Although we begin with a straightforward depiction of believable events in *The Edible Woman*, we soon find ourselves enmeshed in increasing improbability and comic absurdity.

The first of Marion's non-realistic actions is her flight from the bar where she has been spending the evening with Peter, Len and Ainsley. It is Marion's perception of the chase that turns it into a maiden/villain pursuit of Gothic proportions:

> All at once it was no longer a game. The blunt tank-shape was threatening. It was threatening that Peter had not given chase on foot but had enclosed himself in the armour of the car.... (*EW*, p. 73)

> I felt myself caught, set down and shaken. It was Peter, who must have stalked me and waited there on the side-street.... (*EW*, p. 74)

Almost immediately after this, Marion wedges herself under Len's bed thinking of the room as "up there" and feeling "smug" in her "private burrow" (*EW*, p. 76). The purpose of these scenes is twofold. They are, like the wildly extravagant dinner at Duncan's, amusing in an uneasy way. They also serve as dramatizations of Marion's increasing paranoia — Peter's car is a tank; he has "stalked" her; she is an animal in a "burrow." As such they prepare the way for our acceptance of Marion's inability to eat and her final release through the symbolic cake lady. These scenes, then, begin to stretch the realistic fabric of the narrative in order to make a portrayal of the more fantastic truths of the human situation possible. Although Marion's perceptions of herself as hunted victim or tasty morsel about to be devoured are distortions of reality for which she is largely responsible, these perceptions carry a symbolic truth about the general nature of our society and personal relationships. Ours is a consumer society; we feed on each other economically and emotionally.

For a short while Marion's body identifies with all things eaten:

At times when she had meditated on the question she had con-
cluded that the stand it [her body] had taken was an ethical
one: it simply refused to eat anything that had once been, or ...
might still be living. But she faced each day with the forlorn
hope that her body might change its mind. (*EW*, p. 178)

Significantly, she does not agree with her body; she does not want to
hear the squeals of murdered carrots or to hide uneaten meatballs
under lettuce leaves. Hence, the gorgeous cake lady that she ostensibly bakes for Peter is as much for herself. With Peter the cake is
meant as a symbol of his destructive propensities; it is a substitute
for Marion — "I've made you a substitute, something you'll like
much better" (*EW*, p. 271). Marion realizes that the cake is
something of a gamble, however. She is, in fact, testing Peter's surface reality against the cannibalistic reality she perceives beneath his
three-piece suits:

It was easy to see him as normal and safe in the afternoon, but
that didn't alter things. The price of this version of reality was
testing the other one. (*EW*, p. 271)

As a symbol of Peter's reality, the cake fails. He is horrified and
flees. It is Marion who eats this substitute self and in the process is
brought back to consumer reality: "Suddenly she was hungry. Ex-
tremely hungry. The cake after all was only a cake" (*EW*, p. 272).
The disconcerting point, for the reader, is that Marion neither reas-
sesses her opinion of Peter nor appreciates the irony of her own ap-
petite. Instead, she carries on with the job at hand, plunging
"her fork into the carcass, neatly severing the body from the head"
(*EW*, p. 273.)

In addition to the extravagance of scene and the importance of
symbol in *The Edible Woman*, the supporting characters in the novel
are also more and less than realistic fictional portrayals. For the
most part, they are caricatures as Atwood uses the term (see above,
pages 90-91), "outgrowths of their society," distorted and slightly exaggerated. Ainsley, Clara, and the office virgins are variations on
the type of female predator; Len is a typical philanderer; Peter is
tailor-made to be a successful Toronto lawyer. We see them in two-
dimensions and slightly askew through Marion's eyes. Duncan, the
self-indulgent English graduate student, is more important and

92

enigmatic, and in every way the antithesis of Peter — sloppy, ineffectual, childish.

He is invariably there in Marion's life at the end of long walks. After work one evening, she wanders along vaguely in the direction of the park and without surprise finds Duncan. They huddle together on the old bench: " 'You took a long time,' he said quietly at last. 'I've been expecting you' " (*EW*, p. 171). There is no explanation for his remark. Later, after the fiasco of Peter's party and Marion and Duncan's night in a sleazy hotel, they take a long walk through the Toronto ravines together. There Duncan tells her, in his laconic fashion, that she has not 'hatched him into manhood' by sleeping with him; she has merely 'participated in his fantasy life' (*EW*, p. 264), just as he has been participating in hers. It is now time for her "to do something", "to go". He will not help her any further; "it's your own personal cul-de-sac, you invented it, you'll have to think of your own way out" (*EW*, p. 264).

This long fantastic walk through the snowy ravines is symbolic of Marion's psychological position. It is a dead end, a "cul-de-sac" like her relationship with Peter. Now she must act, retrace her steps, or otherwise get out. But who, or what, is Duncan? Friend, enemy, lover? Surrogate or foil for Peter that enables her to see what Peter is? Perhaps "the universal substitute" (*EW*, p. 145)? Or is Duncan another Atwood double, a kind of *doppelgänger*, an objectified part of Marion herself with whom she can commune but who also embodies the narcissism and ruthless egocentricity that she contains? While he irons the clothes she brings him, he gives her his dressing gown to wear and then observes, "you look sort of like me in that" (*EW*, p. 144). As a realistic novel character Duncan is vague. Although he is the opposite of Peter, he is not an alternative. There do not seem to be any viable alternatives in *The Edible Woman*. Duncan is most successful as a symbol of Marion's inner life or subsconscious; he represents her fantasies, her attempts to escape, as well as her sensible return to consumer reality. Duncan knows "mankind cannot bear too much unreality" (*EW*, p. 279). Contrary to T. S. Eliot whose line, "human kind / Cannot bear very much reality" from *Four Quartets*, Duncan bowlderizes, it is not reality but unreality that Marion cannot bear.

The Edible Woman is a skilful and enjoyable exploration of three basic Atwood themes. It is theme, thesis or idea, that is most important for the novel and, in this sense, the novel shares much with traditional satire. Our final response to the book is intellectual where our response to *Surfacing* is emotional. The most obvious theme of *The Edible Woman* is that of consumption. From the title through the tightly unified images of food and eating to the symbolic cake lady, the narrative presents the social, physical, and emotional prevalance of consumerism. Many of the best scenes in the novel take place at table; we do, after all, spend a large part of the day eating. But instead of being a social ritual that brings people together in meaningful, mutually enriching ways, eating becomes a metaphor for economic and emotional cannibalism. Either you eat or are eaten; there are no other choices.

The question of choice is, I feel, a second and more subtle thematic concern. The novel is built upon opposites; to eat or to be eaten is only one example. Peter and Duncan are in every way opposites. Marion herself splits in two as is illustrated by the narrative voice. Major scenes in the book involve either rooms, especially kitchens and dining rooms, or long walks on streets, in parks, or through the ravines. Marion is caught either in an "eddy of present time" or in a pre-determined march of time towards her wedding day. As Duncan tells her during their walk in the ravine, she must "do something." She must act instead of being acted upon. She must refuse to be static and passive, a condition symbolized by the constant use of rooms, and decide to be active. How she should choose to act, however, is problematic because Marion does not have any real alternatives to choose from. Her active walks (and her flight from Peter) are all failed attempts to escape from a condition she inadequately comprehends. Marion is trapped within "the circle game" of her own perception and the "power politics" of our consumer society — the choices resolve themselves into consuming or being consumed, thus, Marion returns to the point from which she began.

The most important theme of *The Edible Woman*, perhaps, is the problem of perception, a problem experienced by Marion and by the reader. The argument, as well as the structure, of the novel, is circular and in this way Atwood thrusts the challenge of perception at us. We are locked within Marion's first person narrative, her perception throughout, until in the final chapter, Duncan suggests that Marion has entirely misunderstood her situation. She explains that she is rid of Peter who was trying to destroy her, to which Duncan responds:

> "That's ridiculous.... Peter wasn't trying to destroy you. That's just something you made up. Actually you were trying to

94

destroy him."

I had a sinking feeling. "Is that true?" I asked. (*EW*, p. 280)

Whether Duncan's explanation is true or false is not clear. We can never know for sure because there is no reliable vantage point outside the closed circle of the narrative from which to take our bearings. As in "Journey to the Interior," "A Compass is useless" and "the movements of the sun /... are erratic." The mixed style of realism, caricature, and romance (fantasy and emphasis on symbol) fully embodies the perceptual conundrum of the book. What is real, what is fantasy? Is Marion's dilemma "just something" she has "made up"? Who knows? Atwood's remarks on the impossibility of writing traditional satire today are instructive here:

> Literature *can* be a mirror, and people *can* recognize themselves in it, and this may lead to change. But in order to write satire in the traditional sense, you must have certain axioms in common with your audience. When something happens in the book that outrages common sense, your audience must agree that it is in fact outrageous.... That's the problem with the century we live in. There's almost nothing you can write about which has not been outdone in absurdity or ghastliness by real events.[8]

Because there are no axioms, no givens, for human behavior or perception, the commonplace and the outrageous, the normal and the abnormal blur and merge. It becomes impossible to distinguish reality and unreality; they are meaningless terms.

And yet *The Edible Woman* does not rest in absurdity for the book carries an ethical burden. The reader, if not Marion, is so placed that he can see beyond the either/or of the novel just far enough to realize that this vicious circle *ought* to be broken; Atwood says "what's important to me is how human beings ought to live and behave."[9] In describing the moral intention of the book, she points out that *The Edible Woman*.

> does make a negative statement about society. In traditional comedy, boy meets girl. There are complications, the complications are resolved and the couple is united. In my book the couple is not united and the wrong couple gets married. The complications are resolved, but not in a way that reaffirms the

social order. The tone of *The Edible Woman* is lighthearted, but in the end it's more pessimistic than *Surfacing*. The difference between them is that *Edible Woman* is a circle and *Surfacing* is a spiral.... the heroine of *Surfacing* does not end where she began.[10]

Chapter VI

Some Kind of Harmony With the World

I think there has to be a third thing again; the ideal would be
somebody who would neither be a killer or a victim, who could
achieve some kind of harmony with the world, which is a
productive or creative harmony.... (Gibson interview, p. 27)

Although Margaret Atwood has said that her novels are all very
different, they raise many of the same questions, psychological,
ethical, social or perceptual. They also share a considerable thematic
and stylistic territory with the poetry. The echoes between the poetry
and the fiction are pleasing and illustrative, especially for her best
novel to date, *Surfacing*. A reader already familiar with *The Circle
Game, Power Politics, Procedures for Underground* and even the
Journals, will orientate very quickly to the landscape of this novel.

That said, however, *Surfacing* must still be discussed as a novel,
a fictional narrative embodying and responding to the conventions,
and our expectations, of the genre. But what kind of novel is it? Both
in Canada and the United States it has been viewed too often as a
treatise — on nationalism by Canadians, on feminism by
Americans. In her interview with Gibson, Atwood called *Surfacing*
"a ghost story" in which she is examining among other things, "the
great Canadian victim complex."[1] Needless to say, Atwood is not
providing a gloss on the novel in the interview; analyzing her writing
is uncongenial to her. Nevertheless, she does give us a number of
useful clues that have been largely ignored. Before attempting to
decide what kind of novel *Surfacing* is or to what extent it is a ghost
story, I would like to examine the text from the usual narrative
points of view — narrative voice, setting, style (language, image,
symbol), structure and, of course, theme. The first (and the last)
question to ask is, what is the story about?

Superficially at least, *Surfacing* has a very simple story. An unnamed protagonist returns to her childhood summer home in the
Laurentians because her father has disappeared. She is accompanied

97

by a lover and two casual friends. Her father is indeed missing, so she begins to search for clues as to his whereabouts; he may be off in the woods, he may have gone mad, or he may be dead. Her friends decide to stay longer than had been planned and this gives the woman time to discover her father's archeological activities and his drowned body. Upset by her loss, she refuses to leave with her friends at the end of the week. She spends a few more days alone on the island during which time she undergoes some terrifying experiences. At the end she is about to answer her lover who has come back to look for her.

As the title implies, the novel is not about surfaces but about depths and the process of rising from those depths. *Surfacing* is not a realistic search for a missing person, but the multi-levelled quest of a contemporary Persephone for a particular type of freedom. On the immediate narrative level of the search for her missing father, the narrator must acknowledge her ties to family and readjust her concept of that thrust for freedom from the family that we all experience. On the psychological, ethical, spiritual, and perceptual levels, the narrator must discover a new way of being, a third way that transcends polarizations, thus enabling the individual to be free of crippling limitations.

The best place to begin a discussion of the novel is at the beginning with the voice that tells us: "I can't believe I'm on this road again...."[2] There is much, also, that the reader must not believe. The voice is a first person singular throughout; the speaker is a nameless young woman. Because we never learn her name or, in fact, very much about her physical appearance, we must perceive her strictly through this voice, and we are as limited to her voice as she is to her own point of view. In a disconcerting sense we cannot say that we know this character with whom we share intense experiences; the voice, though clear, comes from a distance.

This voice is important in several ways. The cool distance of the voice provides an essential emotional control over events as well as dramatizing the cauterized feelings of the speaker — one of the things she must learn to do is to feel. Atwood's use of a first person unnamed speaker draws us into both the novel and the frightening visual world of her protagonist. In fact, it is the voice that creates the claustrophobic atmosphere of the book from which we eventually wish to escape ourselves. Furthermore, this first person voice is a trap. Because it is all we have, we tend to believe the voice until, of course, we discover the elaborate deception at work. We remain locked within the perception of an unreliable narrator, certain only that we cannot let go or trust even though the narrator accepts the fact that she must do both if she is to live. As Atwood points out in her interview with Linda Sandler,

> You have to regard everything my heroine says as the utterance of a fictional character. The reader who endorses the character suddenly finds out that she's been telling horrible lies. The reader ought to be more cautious.[3]

There is no better example of the narrator's limitations than the episode with the "Americans" who turn out to be from Southern Ontario. Rather than question her own position (they have mistaken her for a "Yank") her anger flares outwards: "I was furious with them, they'd disguised themselves" (*Sur*, p. 148). Her opinions are suspect on many other occasions. For example, when David and Anna tell her about the discovery of her father's body she thinks:

> He and Anna glanced at each other: they had planned on hurting me....
> Anna said, "Wouldn't you rather..." and then stopped. They walked back down the steps, disappointed both of them, their trap had failed. (*Sur*, p. 180)

Because the narrator is so thoroughly trapped in her own position and a master of false histories and roles herself, she assumes that others are equally untrustworthy. In this instance her assessment is probably false. How accurately has she ever seen Joe?

This type of narrative voice is essential to *Surfacing*. Only because we are firmly located within her perceptions are we able to share the narrator's subsequent visionary experience. The gradual narrative shift from the realism of direct address, colloquial language, and the sense of character etiology, into a highly symbolic style informed by mythic pattern is facilitated by this choice of voice. Despite the obvious advantages, however, there are problems. The first is the tone of the voice which remains detached and authoritative throughout. The narrator never expresses feeling which is, after all, what she seeks, and has presumably rediscovered by the end of the novel. This may be explained by a failure of language, or by the fact that she is only on the *brink* of acting as a whole sentient human being as the novel closes. The authority of this voice is troublesome as well: how can we be sure that she has achieved anything by the end when her basic perceptions of phenomena are suspect throughout. It is not enough to say that we must accept her perceptions because they are phenomenologically true for her; the narrative moves out from private truth towards ethics and social criticism.

Still more perplexing is the tense of the narrative voice. In Parts I and III, the narrator speaks in the present while, in Part II, she speaks in the past. Possibly Atwood wishes to emphasize both the narrator's self-alienation and her important journey into her past with the past tense, and the sense of immediate felt experience with the present. The purpose of Part II is to carry the narrator into her past until the earliest image of her drowning brother fuses with the more recent abortion and the present moment of finding her father's corpse. In that moment discrete time is annihilated as she perceives the truth in a temporal continuum. In fact, this is one of the major ordeals facing the heroine. She has set up neat temporal divisions in her life for self-defense only to discover that she has cut herself off from her context in time. During the important purging scene in Part III during which she symbolically destroys borders, limits, and artificial boundaries, she admits that,

> Everything from history must be eliminated, the circles and the arrogant square pages.... It is time that separates us, I was a coward, I would not let them into my age, my place. Now I must enter theirs. (*Sur*, p. 205)

Although I can appreciate the purpose for a past tense voice in Part II, the tense shift nevertheless violates the temporal sequence of the narrative. We move with the narrator from day one in the present to, approximately, day twelve in the present; from what conceivable point in time does the narration in Part II take place? Margaret Laurence faced a similar problem with the past in *The Diviners*, but she solved it more convincingly by using a constant past voice as a base for present memories. The temporal shift in *Surfacing* remains contrived.

One of the problems in *The Edible Woman* is what Atwood called the preposterousness of "symbolism in a realistic context."[4] This is also a major stylistic, hence thematic, challenge in *Surfacing* From the start, voice and language co-operate to produce an increasingly symbolic text. Atwood's approach is phenomenological.

She uses language to present the object seen in its utmost clarity. The cumulative effect is that words or objects seen acquire an importance that forces us to respond and to interpret them metaphorically.

An example of this shift from perceived object to metaphor is obvious in the description of the heron:

> It was behind me, I smelled it before I saw it; then I heard the flies. The smell was like decaying fish. I turned around and it was hanging upside down by a thin blue nylon rope tied round its feet and looped over a tree branch, its wings fallen open. It looked at me with its mashed eye. (*Sur*, p. 133)

Beginning with the indefinite pronoun, "It," we are thrust into an unknown situation which we must experience, through our senses. The bird is presented with vivid simplicity through smell, sound, and sight. The position of the bird, the nylon rope, its wings, while capturing a precise visual image, suggest further resonances of victimization, vulnerability, and the destructive impact of the artificial on the natural — the "thin blue nylon rope" around its feet and the tree. The bird's "mashed eye," because it is so pictorially graphic and disgusting, emphasizes the vulnerability of sight on the one hand, its terrible power on the other; the image functions in much the same way as the fish hook and open eye of the prefacing poem in *Power Politics*. The question of visual perception is central in *Surfacing*, for the heroine must learn to "see" in order to be whole. In passages like this she (with the reader) is led to visual perception through the more highly contextual senses of smell and hearing in order to fully experience the impact of the moment.

Language, as the heroine knows, is important: "a language is everything you do" (*Sur*, p. 148). And the language in *Surfacing* says much about the narrator. It is cool, precise, almost surgical; the narrator wields it like a knife to slice away her friends' facades, and finally her own. This impersonal, economical style maintains a crucial control over the rising hysteria of experience, as well as conveying, very successfully, the narrator's cerebral approach to life, her inability to feel. Through the language we are held at an emotional remove from the speaker much as she holds herself apart from life, while the frequently fragmented sentence structure suggests the disjunct and alienated perspective from which she views her world:

Nothing is the same, I don't know the way any more. I slide

my tongue around the ice cream, trying to concentrate on it, they put seaweed in it now, but I'm starting to shake, why is the road different, he shouldn't have allowed them to do it, I want to turn around and go back to the city and never find out what happened to him. I'll start crying, that would be horrible, none of them would know what to do and neither would I. I bite down into the cone and I can't feel anything for a minute but the knife-hard pain up the side of my face. Anesthesia, that's one technique: if it hurts invent a different pain. I'm all right. (*Sur*, p. 13)

The sentence pattern here reflects one of the narrator's main responses to life — a statement of fact, she is lost, followed by a series of individual syntactic units that accumulate to suggest her disorientation. Because she cannot meaningfully connect her responses, she attempts to annihilate the pain of emotional confusion with a physical pain. The emotional and syntactic pattern apparent in this single paragraph is representative of the movement of the book as a whole and of the narrator's dilemma. She repeatedly acknowledges a fact of her existence, faces her confusion, and then attempts to retreat into an alternate surface fact or an alternate safe version of her life. It is a pattern of diving and surfacing that will climax in an actual dive at the end of Part II when she finally agrees to forego anesthesia.

Imagery and symbolism in the book, while diverse and rich, have a stunning clarity of function and focus. I feel that it is in terms of image and symbol that *Surfacing* most succeeds. The image patterns, finally they are symbols, that I would like to examine are the central ones of 'character,' the landscape, the body, mirrors, and water. In each instance the metaphoric intention is the same — to express the limitations and possibilities of duality.

Because we must see the world strictly through the eyes of our narrator, the other characters gradually take on symbolic, instead of realistic, importance. Thus, David and Anna are opposites: he cannot feel; she can. Furthermore, David is, in the narrator's view, "an imposter, a pastiche" with "Secondhand American... spreading over him in patches, like mange or lichen" (*Sur*, p. 174), and Anna is an equally false symbol of our destructive society — a sterile doll, a Playboy centerfold. Joe is little more than raw material only partially, awkwardly, shaped like his pots; he serves the narrator's immediate physical purpose. Even her parents are opposite sides of an equation. Her father represents the forces of reason and logic; he is

102

the head. Her mother embodies the intuitional, instinctual realm of gesture and feeling; she is the body. Her father's gift is the truth (he was always ruthless about the truth) of her abortion discovered when she sees his body; paradoxically his death also reveals the failure of his logic — one cannot photograph the gods. Her mother's gift is organic and contextual, a picture of a baby in its mother's womb. The narrator, of course, cannot be complete herself until she has rediscovered both parents *and* re-established them in the context of her life.

Most important is the baby, not simply another "Great Canadian Baby" as Atwood describes them in *Survival*, but a symbol integral to the development and focus of the book. Even before she has admitted the fact, the "pure logic" of her abortion, the narrator knows that she is incomplete:

> No hints or facts, I didn't know when it had happened. I must have been all right then; but after that I'd allowed myself to be cut in two. Woman sawn apart in a wooden crate, wearing a bathing suit, smiling, a trick done with mirrors, I read it in a comic book; only with me there had been an accident and I came apart. The other half, the one locked away, was the only one that could live; I was the wrong half, detached, terminal I was nothing but a head, or, no, something minor like a severed thumb; numb. (*Sur*, p. 124)

Quite simply, she has taken the logical to its extreme. Unable to cope with her feelings, she has cauterized them and attempted to live through her mind alone. In the crucial diving scene, the body of her father fuses with the image of her drowned brother and the memory of her aborted fetus; a connection is made, a context established whereby she can begin to understand both the damage she has suffered and caused. The conception of another child symbolizes reparation, fusion of opposites in a new context, and her own re-birth:

> He trembles and then I can feel my lost child surfacing within me, forgiving me, rising from the lake where it has been prisoned for so long, its eyes and teeth phosphorescent; the two halves clasp, interlocking like fingers, it buds, it sends out fronds. (*Sur*, p. 187)

The landscape of the novel is, of course, both literal and metaphorical. In a sense, the narrator is the isolated island they are

103

on, surrounded by the lake "blue and cool as redemption" (*Sur*, p. 16). Not until she can break down the distorting barriers between self and other, or until she can leave the island to immerse herself in the water, can she hope to establish a new complete self. The narrator's problem is that she can embrace neither extreme without denying her humanity. To remain on her island of self is to be enclosed in a bottle, reduced only to an unreliable visual sense:

> At some point my neck must have closed over, pond freezing or a wound, shutting me into my head; since then everything had been glancing off me, it was like being in a vase, or the village where I could see them but not hear because I couldn't understand what was being said. Bottles distort for the observer too: frogs in the jam jar stretched wide, to them watching I must have appeared grotesque. (*Sur*, p. 121)

But to leave the self entirely, to fuse with the other, is madness. During her ordeal she feels that she is first "a tree leaning," and then "a place" (*Sur*, p. 210), before she admits: "I have to get up, I get up. Through the ground, break surface, I'm standing now; separate again" (*Sur*, p. 211). By the end of the book she knows she must use language, "the intercession of words," and that she must "live in the usual way" (*Sur*, p. 220).

Water is established in Chapter I as the entrance to redemption and it carries that symbolic weight throughout the book. It is by diving to find the pictographs that she discovers her father's corpse and releases her drowned truth. Later she purges herself in the water, being careful to "dip my head beneath the water, washing my eyes" and "leaving my false body floated on the surface" (*Sur*, p. 206). Water transforms her as it will her baby ("a goldfish now in my belly, undergoing its watery changes," *Sur*, p. 222), making it possible for her to experience the visions of her parents and, hence, to understand their significance as parts of herself. Water is important as the entrance to redemption and as the medium of metamorphosis, but it is finally only water, quiet like the trees, non-human, insufficient, "asking and giving nothing."

The two most familiar Atwood images for alienation are mirrors and parts of the body. The protagonist is fascinated by disjunct parts of the body, arms without hands, "the cut-off pieces of early martyrs" (*Sur*, p. 29). She sees herself as a severed head or finger, and remembers the obscene drawings in a tugboat:

> I was shocked, not by those parts of the body, we'd been told about those, but that they should be cut off like that from the bodies that ought to have gone with them, as though they could detach themselves and crawl around on their own like snails.
>
> (*Sur*, p. 138)

The images serve as reminders of the destructive way we live by separating ourselves from our environments, our bodies, other people, and finally even ourselves. As the narrator points out in reference to the heron, "the only relation" one can have to a living creature that is viewed as a separate object is "to destroy it." Mirrors, like snapshots or the movie "Random Samples," reveal the hideousness of fragmentation and entrapment. The narrator perceives Anna's soul as trapped in her compact mirror just as her body is trapped by the celluloid image in the camera. The narrator will destroy the movie and turn the mirror in the cabin to the wall in the effort to free Anna and herself from the false and artificial selves reflected there. When she finally looks in the mirror after her ordeal, it is to see what she will become if she refuses a human context — and the mirror tells the truth.

Surfacing is written in three parts, each part representing a stage in the protagonist's search for her father, for herself. Time moves in a simple chronological manner covering approximately twelve days, two days in Part I, a week in Part II, and another few days in Part III. The three part structure carries the plot from an opening condition to an antidote for that condition to, thirdly, a new condition; the protagonist moves from a superficial harmony that merely disguises her true alienation through a traumatizing exploration of her position, to a new and more hopeful wholeness in the final section of the book. The narrative moves both horizontally, straight forward in time, and vertically, deeper and deeper into the past paralleling the descent of the narrator into the lake and forest.

As I suggested earlier, the descent-ascent pattern follows the paradigm of the Persephone myth, a myth that Atwood has found attractive from her earliest poetry on. The narrator, a Persephone figure, must not only experience the underworld before returning to her Mother, but her descent also leads to the knowledge that she must henceforth embody *both* worlds; never again can she inhabit one or the other. This acceptance of duality, basic to the myth, informs each level of the narrative.

In order to make the shape of the book, descent to ascent, credible, Atwood creates an incremental rhythm swinging between fic-

105

tional present and memory that starts very slowly and gradually builds to the diving climax of Part II. Her memories begin to surface tentatively; she recalls the car sickness she felt as a child when her father hurtled over the old road and her mother handed out Lifesavers, but she shuts out the memory by calling her family "'they' as if they were somebody else's family" (*Sur*, p. 13). Early in Chapter II her memories are longer and more intense; she leans over the bridge and the rush of the water brings back the memory of a dangerous canoe trip (*Sur*, pp. 18-19). From this point on, her memories gather momentum. At the close of chapter III, she recalls the important near-drowning of her brother (*Sur*, p. 35). As the narrative proceeds we move, with the protagonist, deeper into her mind and past, leaving objective surroundings and the present increasingly behind.

By the time the narrator dives to find the submerged pictographs we are prepared to expect something extraordinary. She makes three major discoveries, her father's corpse, the damaging truth of her abortion, and her need to keep diving in order to surface. Instead of being the climax, this revelation only marks the beginning of a still more extraordinary descent. Part II closes with three short paragraphs again spoken in the present tense. The dive into time is over; now she must immerse herself in space, "the truth is here" (*Sur*, p. 197).

Various ways have been used to describe the visionary events of Part III in *Surfacing*, from psychological to religious, from Laing to Eliade and "rite de passage" myth.[5] More likely Atwood is drawing upon Ojibway concepts of homology and transformation. Basically what the narrator experiences is the metamorphosis from self to non-self, other, or place. Atwood has said that she does not believe in the ego; for Atwood "the self is a place in which things happen... where experiences intersect."[6] By becoming, momentarily, "the thing in which the trees and animals move and grow,... a place" (*Sur*, p. 210), the narrator is able to experience, first the vision of her mother, then the more terrifying vision of her father:

I say Father.

He turns toward me and it's not my father. It is what my father saw, the thing you meet when you've stayed here too long alone.

When I go to the fence the footprints are there, side by side in the mud. My breath quickens, it was true, I saw it. But the

106

prints are too small, they have toes; I place my feet in them and find that they are my own. (*Sur*, pp. 216-217)

What she sees, if you will, is herself, her mother and father as elements of herself and this place. What she learns is that total immersion, like innocence, is only one way "only one kind of truth, one hand" (*Sur*, p. 220):

> No total salvation, resurrection, Our father, Our mother, I pray, Reach down for me, but it won't work: they dwindle, grow, become what they were, human. Something I never gave them credit for; but their totalitarian innocence was my own. (*Sur*, p. 220)

The narrator has first tried to live on the surface, cut off from herself, her past, her place, and others. Realizing the inadequacy of this amnesiac condition, she gradually descends "back to the past, inside the skull, is it the same place" [sic] (p. 219), only to find that this immersion, while cleansing and illuminating, is not the final answer either; one cannot insulate oneself in a hard shell of logic, nor can one become entirely alogical, non-human, other. These opposites must be reconciled in a third option. As Atwood says in the interview with Gibson:

> I think there has to be a third thing again; the ideal would be somebody who would neither be a killer or a victim, who could achieve some kind of harmony with the world, which is a productive or creative harmony.... Now in neither book [*The Edible Woman* and *Surfacing*] is that actualized, but in both it's seen as a possibility finally, whereas initially it is not.[7]

What the narrator in *Surfacing* has rediscovered is the context for herself and the destructiveness of opposites. She is prepared to *start* loving, talking, trusting, establishing an extensive context that will include others.

At the beginning of this discussion of *Surfacing* I said that the narrator was on a multi-levelled quest for freedom, but the freedom she is looking for is not the individualistic drive 'to set out for the territory ahead.' Her quest for freedom can only end with her acceptance or rediscovery of her context or place, psychic and physical. Like Persephone, her mythical counterpart, freedom does not lie in escape. She will be free only when she can establish her relationship with her place, family, past, friends and self. When Joe comes alone to find her at the end of the novel, she recognizes his significance: "what's important is that he's here, a mediator, an ambassador, offering me something: captivity in any of its forms, a new freedom?" (*Sur*, p. 223)

Epistemologically, as so often in the poetry, Atwood presents us with the question — how do we know or perceive ourselves and others? Once again, a speaker must learn how to see. In order to know the truth, the narrator in *Surfacing* must experience vision or hallucination, she must experience a oneness with place that normal vision, which divides and separates, never permits. She sees the world including herself first as objects, random samples, then as without boundaries or fences, as pure being. Having seen life from both extremes she may be able to free herself from the limitations of both. Spiritually, the narrator is searching for her Gods, not Jesus, but her personal Gods, the Gods of her place. These, she finds, are her ancestors — "Our father, Our mother" (*Sur*, p. 220). Having found them she realizes she must relinquish them "defining them by their absence"(*Sur*, p. 220). In other words, she must trust, have faith, instead of retreating into doubt and fear.

In addition to being an epistemological and religious quest, *Surfacing* is also a social and psychological one. Socially the result seems similar to that in many Canadian novels from Connor to Laurence. In order to be truly free, the narrator cannot stay on her island shut off from mankind. She must return, "reenter my own time" bringing with her "from the distant past five nights ago the time-traveller, the primeval one" (*Sur*, p. 222). Not only must she return to society and normalcy, she must bring what she has learned with her:

This above all, to refuse to be a victim. Unless I can do that I can do nothing. I have to recant, give up the old belief that I am powerless and because of it nothing I can do will ever hurt anyone. A lie which was always more disastrous than the truth would have been. The word games, the winning and losing games are finished; at the moment there are no others but they will have to be invented, withdrawing is no longer possible and the alternative is death. (*Sur*, p. 222)

Although *Surfacing* is not a treatise on feminism or nationalism, it is a highly moral book. By acknowledging her abortion as destructive, she, in fact, accepts the responsibility of passivity, the evil of so-called innocence, the hypocrisy of living self-withdrawn in order to avoid injury to oneself or to another. To live as if life were a war to be won or lost is wrong, whether you destroy or acquiesce in destruction; the third way of living, the "productive or creative harmony," can only be invented when one is free of the victor/victim opposites.

Finally, *Surfacing* is a psychological quest and it is on this level that we have a ghost story. Speaking of ghost stories to Graeme Gibson Atwood remarks:

> You can have the Henry James kind, in which the ghost that one sees is in fact a fragment of one's own self which has split off, and that to me is the most interesting kind and that is obviously the tradition I'm working in.[8]

The parts of the narrator's self that have "split off," her *doppelgängers*, are her aborted baby and her parents. She will not be free of these ghosts until she recognizes them and readmits them into her psychic and emotional life. This idea of the ghostly self or *doppelgänger* is important to the psychological level of the book in yet another way. In his essay "Atwood Gothic" from *Another Time*, Eli Mandel points out that:

> In folklore, the doppelganger [sic] motif, in which one meets oneself coming back as one goes forward, signifies either death or the onset of prophetic power.[9]

Just before the narrator of *Surfacing* begins her crucial dive, she 'meets herself' in the water: "My other shape was in the water, not my reflection but my shadow, foreshortened, outline blurred, rays streaming out from around my head" (*Surf*, p. 1611). The sight of this other self (*dopplegängers* are often spoken of as shadows) suggests the importance of the dive: it is dangerous, she could drown, but instead she experiences a vision. This shadow "signifies ... the onset of prophetic power."

By the end of *Surfacing*, the narrator has succeeded in her quest; she has found what she needs to begin a new, complete and free life. Whether or not she will create this new life is entirely open, but at least possible, in the closing lines of the text. Whether the book succeeds as a unified multi-levelled quest is another question. The book strains, I feel, under the effort to fuse psychological and social (or ethical) quests with religious and epistemological ones. The immediate level of the narrative, the search for a missing father, as well as the mythological paradigm, carry the psychological and social burden of the theme more convincingly than either of the other two aspects of the quest. Furthermore the succinct, almost abrupt, moralizing of Chapters XXVI and XXVII, while focussing the personal and social ethics of the novel, is an anti-climax to the preceding mystical experiences; the shift from metamorphosis or metaphor to axiom — "To prefer life, I owe them that" — is incommensurate with the intensity of vision. However, these weaknesses of the narrative, as well as the somewhat awkward shift in voice tense from present to past to present, do not seriously impair what remains a beautiful and powerful work. Margaret Atwood's command of language and image, her ability to control and shape the narrative, make *Surfacing* a finely wrought work of contemporary fiction.

Chapter VII

More Than a Very Double Life

> This was the beginning of my double life. But hadn't my
> life always been double? There was always that shadowy
> twin, thin when I was fat, fat when I was thin,... But not
> twin even, for I was more than double, I was triple, mul-
> tiple, and now I could see that there was more than one
> life to come, there were many. (*LO*, p. 246)

If *The Edible Woman* is an anti-comedy and *Surfacing* is a ghost
story, then *Lady Oracle* must be an anti-Gothic — and it is, that and
much more. Anti-Gothic is Atwood's descriptive term for her third
novel which she links to the treatment of Gothic in Jane Austen's
Northanger Abbey.[1] As a parody of the Gothic novel, *Lady Oracle*
comments upon the tradition rising in the late 18th century, notably
with Ann Radcliffe's *Mysteries of Udolpho*, and continuing in the
19th century with the Brontës and Rider Haggard. Atwood, who has
taught the 19th century British novel and studied Haggard, knows
the subject well.[2] So does Joan Delacourt/Foster.

Although these nineteenth century Gothic roots are important to
Lady Oracle and must be discussed further, the novel has other
relatives both older and contemporary. *Lady Oracle*, with its self-
dramatizing heroine, Joan, poised between social realities and fan-
tastic escapes, recalls the intrepid adventures in Defoe's *Moll
Flanders* and the world of risk and manipulation in Richardson's
Pamela. As a parody of Gothic romance *Lady Oracle*, as well as the
costume Gothics that Joan writes, are hilarious facsimiles of Harlequin romances. On a more serious artistic level, however, *Lady
Oracle* shares much with contemporary works such as J.P.
Donleavy's *The Beastly Beatitudes of Balthazar B.*, Donald
Barthelme's *Snow White*, John Barth's *Lost in the Funhouse*, or cer-
tains films by Lina Wertmuller and Fellini (*Swept Away* or *The End
of the world...* and *Juliet of the Spirits*, for example). In common
with Donleavy and Wertmuller are the unsettling mixture of humour
and sadness, the sense of self-reflexive satire or self-parody, the confusion between life and art or social realities and imaginative plots

and a final sense not so much of ambiguity as of inconclusiveness. The extent to which Atwood's novel resembles *Snow White* is more limited. Where *Snow White* is a bawdy parody of the fairy tale, *Lady Oracle*'s use of the genre is lighter. The resemblance between *Lady Oracle* and Barth's *Funhouse* (in narrative voice, use of myth and concept of duplication) highlights the parallels between the contemporary American use of fantasy and picaresque and trends in contemporary Canadian fiction apparent in Robert Kroetsch and Jack Hodgins, as well as Atwood.

Although *Lady Oracle* is a funny book, a veritable feast of verbal wit and comic situation, it is not simple. Part of Atwood's achievement is that she has examined "the perils of gothic thinking"[3] in an amusing yet serious treatment of popular literary forms and stereotypes. At the same time, she offers a combination of parody and satire that results in that seriocomic tone referred to above. In terms of her own work, *Lady Oracle* most closely resembles *The Edible Woman* with its mixture of parody, satire and comedy. Its relationship to *Surfacing* is less obvious but more intriguing. What happens after one surfaces from the impurities of Lake Ontario? Well, read *Lady Oracle* to find out.

Lady Oracle went through five drafts and required two years to complete. It was first cast as a second person address to Arthur and was to end, tragically, with a real death.[4] The book grew and changed immensely in the process of writing, until it became the autobiography of Joan Delacourt, wife of Arthur Foster and writer of Costume Gothics. Joan tells her story, in part to the reporter who has discovered her, but chiefly to us.

The story opens with this startling announcement: "I planned my death carefully."[5] Joan has indeed staged her drowning in Lake Ontario and is hiding in the small Italian town of Terremoto — the town of earthquakes. The brief first part of the novel takes place entirely in the present at Terremoto and quickly introduces us to Joan's personality, her need for escape, her lurid imagination and her writing. Why she is hiding out or has staged her death and left her husband, only unfolds slowly in the three subsequent parts of the novel that cover, in chronological order, the snarl of Joan's several lives. She had wanted her death, unlike her life, "to be neat and simple, understated, even a little severe" (*LO*, p. 7), but her love of plots, and a recalcitrant real world, have conspired to expose her. Her story, *apologia*-cum-confession, is told after the fact for, as we learn in the final section of the book, Joan's retreat has been discovered by a reporter whom she has knocked on the head with a Cinzano bottle. While he recuperates in hospital, she explains.

Joan spends a miserable childhood and adolescence in Toronto suburbia as a fat child, the despair of her beautiful, social-climbing mother. Her father, an anaesthetist and veteran of World War II, is seldom present. The more her mother pushes her to conform, the more Joan eats. Food is her means of defiance and escape because, as a fat girl, she is immune from the normal tribulations of adolescence; she is simply ignored. As a child, Joan is scarred by two events, a ballet recital at seven and persecution while a Brownie.

Rotund little Joan longs for the closing performances of her ballet school because she will be able to dance as a beautiful butterfly with wings: the adult Joan tells us — "I was hoping for magic transformations, even then" (*LO*, p. 46). The only magic she experiences, unfortunately, is the expedient trickery of the "Miss Flegg Syndrome": "if you're going to be made to look ridiculous and there's no way out of it, you may as well pretend you meant to" (*LO*, p. 48). The ballet teacher, Miss Flegg, realizes that Joan is a ludicrous butterfly and transforms her, instead, into a mothball. Her improvised part consists of stomping about among the dainty butterflies in a fuzzy white sack. Despite the popularity of her performance, the child feels heartbroken and betrayed. Still attracted by the magic of wings, Joan joins Brownies where the clever girls "fly up" to Girl Guides and where "frowns and scowls make ugly things. Smiling gives them fairy " 'wings' " (*LO*, p. 58). Once again she is betrayed. This time vicious Brownies leave Joan tied to a post in a ravine where bad men lurk. She is rescued by a man whom she confuses with "the daffodil man," an exhibitionist she had seen earlier:

> I still wasn't sure, though: was it the daffodil man or not? Was the man who untied me a rescuer or a villain? Or, an even more baffling thought: was it possible for a man to be both at once? (*LO*, p. 64)

This episode encourages Joan's talent for casting people, particularly men, in roles. Furthermore, these instances of transformation become touchstones in Joan's life. Her desire to dance, her longing for magic wings, and her belief in daffodil men who mask "long sharp teeth like icicles" recur, always with disastrous results. As she grows, Joan withdraws deeper into protective layers of fat practising the "Miss Flegg syndrome" in order to defy her mother:

I swelled visibly, relentlessly, before her very eyes, I rose like dough, my body advanced inch by inch towards her across the dining-room table, in this at least I was undefeated. I was five feet four and still growing, and I weighed a hundred and eighty-two pounds. (*LO*, p. 70)

Perverse though it may be, Joan achieves an undeniable transformation.

The main influence in Joan's life during her teens, apart from her mother, is her Aunt Lou. Through this beloved aunt, Joan discovers maudlin Hollywood movies, the oddities of the Canadian National Exhibition, and Leda Sprott's spiritualism. She begins to have haunting dreams of a fat lady, first seen at the CNE, in pink tutu and dancing slippers. The most significant of her experiences with Aunt Lou is her discovery of spiritualism and automatic writing. Events at the Jordan Chapel where transformation (" 'we will emerge with beautiful wings; we will be butterflies, and fly up toward the sun' " *LO*, p. 107), mystery and the supernatural are tailor-made to appeal to Joan's imagination, reappear throughout her life in most improbable ways. It is Leda Sprott's suggestion that she try automatic writing which later leads to the poems in "Lady Oracle," and the terms Joan uses to describe her own death and rebirth echo the spiritualist jargon.

Aunt Lou affects Joan in two further ways. She leaves Joan two thousand dollars in her will on the sole condition that her niece lose one hundred pounds. Because Joan is desperate to escape from her mother, she diets in earnest until, transformed into a slim red-haired beauty, she is free to fly to England: "This was the formal beginning of my second self" (*LO*, p. 137), Joan tells us. By chance she meets a Polish Count as her money is running out, and it is with Paul that she learns to write escape fiction — his are nurse romances, hers Costume Gothics. She chooses her late Aunt's name, Louisa K. Delacourt, as her pen-name. By this time Joan's life is complicated. In fact, it is already beginning to resemble a Gothic plot. She abandons her Count without explanation (a revolver she discovered while snooping in his room makes her unwilling to confront him) in order to move in with Arthur Foster, an *afficionado* of current causes.

One day she returns to the apartment to find her mother's astral body awaiting her. This apparition presages her mother's death which necessitates her return in Toronto. Some months later she is rejoined by Arthur, they marry, and Joan continues to keep her past fatness and present writing career secret because she has "decided that passionate revelation scenes were better avoided and that hidden depths should remain hidden; facades were at least as truthful" (*LO*, p. 197).

If Joan seemed an unlikely candidate for a heroine as a chubby child or an obese adolescent, she seems even less likely a choice as the wife of the prosaic Arthur. But as Jane Austen emphasizes in the opening pages of *Northanger Abbey*, "when a young lady is to be an heroine... something must and will happen to throw a hero in her way."[6] Joan begins to experiment with candles, mirrors and automatic writing in order to work out an occult scene in her current Costume Gothic. Although she abandons the practice after a few months, she decides to publish her scribblings as a book of poetry. This book, called "Lady Oracle," bears striking resemblance to earlier episodes in Joan's life — the daffodil man, Joan's fascination with wings, her lasting affection for Tennyson's *Lady of Shallot*, and indelible memories of her terrifying mother:

> *She sits on the iron throne*
> *She is one and three*
> *Tha dark lady   the redgold lady*
> *the blank lady   oracle*
> *of blood, she who must be*
> *obeyed   forever*
> *Her glass wings are gone*
> *She floats down the river*
> *singing her last song (LO, p. 226)*

Joan Foster is an instant publishing success, a "culture heroine." Arthur is unhappy, however, because the poems are critical of marriage and sexual politics. At a publisher's party Joan meets the Royal Porcupine, a "con-create" poet. With his red beard, green eyes, fantastic hats and cloaks, he sweeps Joan away into the fifth dimension. She has found her hero.

Unfortunately, the Royal Porcupine, also known as Chuck Brewer, falls in love with Joan and wants to live a normal life with her. For Joan this spells disaster, the loss of her fantasy life, her escape from the "soggy domestic atmosphere" of home, and above all the diminishment of her hero:

> But I didn't want him to spoil things, I didn't want him to become gray and multi-dimensional and complicated like

everyone else. Was every Heathcliff a Linton in disguise?
(*LO*, p. 269).

Events follow each other rapidly. Joan receives threats which may be from Chuck, Paul reappears ready to whisk her away, and she begins to be blackmailed by a local parasite. Under these pressures she decides to escape. She plans to stage her drowning and then slip away to Italy.

Joan's life and *Lady Oracle* are scrolled and festooned "like the frame of a baroque mirror" (*LO*, p. 70). Atwood has created numerous characters and three separate settings, Toronto, London, Terremoto, with precise realistic detail. The narrative, however, is more than the chronological presentation of events and people in Joan's life. Interspersed with the main story are several passages from *Stalked by Love*, the Gothic Joan has been writing at the time of her 'death'. These passages, delightful examples of Gothic writing at its worst, function as crazy mirrors for the main story; Joan's life is as fantastic and melodramatic as her Costume Gothics. *Stalked by Love* functions as a mirror within *Lady Oracle* in still another way. The more we learn about the novel, the more apparent it is that the intrepid heroine Charlotte and the passionate evil wife Felicia, who has long red hair, green eyes, and small teeth, are reflections of Joan herself. Furthermore, as Joan's story reaches its climax, with Joan pursued by threatening males, executing daring escapes, and terrified by approaching footsteps, it becomes fused (or confused) with *Stalked by Love*. The parallels are dramatic:

> *She took hold of the doorknob and turned it. The door unlocked and swung outward.... There, standing on the threshold, waiting for her, was Redmond.... Then she knew. Redmond was the killer. (Stalked by love, LO, p. 342)*
>
> But if I turned the handle the door would unlock and swing outward, and I would have to face the man who stood waiting for me, for my life.
>
> I opened the door. I knew who it would be. (*LO*, p. 343)

Joan has entered the mirror of her own creation. In a gesture typical of a true Gothic heroine she smashes the villain over the head, only to discover that he is not, after all, a villain.

Lady Oracle does not end on that heroic note. The unconscious reporter covered in blood brings Joan back to reality. Atwood does not allow her heroine, honour sullied, to redeem herself in death, nor does she allow her to fall into the arms of her true love. Instead, Joan will return to Toronto to clear the friends who are charged with her murder and to confess all. She knows she "should learn some lesson from all of this" (*LO*, p. 345). The extent of her lesson, however, seems to be that she will stop writing Costume Gothics — "I think they were bad for me" — and "try some science fiction" (*LO*, p. 345). Apparently, she will relinquish one form of escapism for another.

It is doubtful that Joan has progressed at all. It is also possible that Joan has lied throughout. She tells us that her story does not contain "very many" lies, but earlier in her tale she describes herself as a "compulsive and romantic" liar (*LO*, p. 148) who has "fabricated" her life "time after time" because "the truth was not convincing" (*LO*, p. 150). Once again Atwood has created a first person narrator who is locked within her own story. Marion's story comes full circle, leaving her where she began. The narrator in *Surfacing* appears to spiral out of herself into a degree of fresh awareness. Joan Foster's life, however, like her story, is neither a circle nor a spiral; it is a maze.

In order to enter the maze of *Lady Oracle*, one must be familiar with the rituals of Gothic romance and fairy tales. With either the Gothic novels of such 18th century British writers as Mrs. Radcliffe and Monk Lewis or contemporary Harlequin Romances, the basic type of fiction is the same. These works are romances, whether or not their characters wear costumes and move through the predictable events of their lives in some distant age and exotic setting. In a recent example, the virtuous, intrepid (though otherwise quite ordinary) heroine, dashes around contemporary "jetset" New York, Paris and London until — the villain's "fingers" close around her throat and "the scream dies on her lips."[7] The plot races to its conclusion as the hero rescues the heroine in a remote English cottage with central heating and picture windows!

These romances rely chiefly on plot. There is a predictable series of events involving death, threats of deaths or rape to the heroine, the inevitable confusion in her mind between the hero and the villain, narrow escapes and breathless chases, all resulting in rescues and happy endings. The world portrayed in Gothic romance is melodramatic and simplistic. Exaggerated or fantastic experiences occur, possibly including a flirtation with supernatural forces, but all ends happily, right wins over wrong, virtue is rewarded, and the hero and heroine marry. The characters are two-dimensional portrayals of good or bad. The heroine, usually fair-haired, delicate but courageous, has her opposite in a dark lady who represents cruelty, cunning, avarice, jealousy and sensuality. The hero and villain are comparable, and there is ultimately no difficulty in deciding who should live or die, who should be rewarded or punished.

Gothic romance offers a world of vicarious danger, titillation and escape, but it exploits the idea of the helpless female object at the mercy of superior male forces. Although Joan recognizes the exploitative nature of her writing, she values the need for escape. Joan herself longs for happy endings and "the simplicity of that world, where happiness was possible and wounds were only ritual ones" (*LO*, p. 284). It *may* be true, as Northrop Frye argues, that all literature comes from other literature — *Lady Oracle* parodies the very idea — but life does not, or should not, especially if that literature is Gothic romance. In her "lust for happy endings" and simplicity, Joan repeatedly confuses reality with romance. When Paul suggests that she run away with him, romantic scenarios tempt her: "He swam before me in a haze of nostalgia. Was this my love, my rescuer?" (*LO*, p. 280) Shortly after this meeting, as she soaks in the bathtub with Paul's latest nurse novel, she hears the proverbial "definite footsteps" and freezes with fear; "visions of knife-wielding rapists, their fangs dripping blood" (*LO*, p. 284), flash before her. The intruder is only Frazer Buchanan in tweed jacket.

Fairy tales share much with Gothic romance — damsels in distress, threatening villains, shining rescuers. An important distinction between the two is that where the romance provides escape from reality, the fairy tale usually develops an escape from enchantment with a reassertion of the real nature of things. Cinderella can marry a prince or the ugly toad marry the princess because they are noble and beautiful to begin with, in real life as it were. As Iona and Peter Opie point out in *The Classic Fairy Tales:*

> The transformation is not an actual transformation but a disenchantment, the breaking of a spell. In each case we are aware that the person was always noble, that the magic has wrought no change in the person's soul, only in his or her outward form.[8]

In the case of our heroine, her desire for "magic transformations" and new lives is basically escapist. From blob to sex object, from blackmail victim to carefree tourist "striding with laughing teeth into an aqua sea" (*LO*, p. 7), Joan wants to discard the past.

Nevertheless, she *has* fallen under an evil spell, a transformation of the fairy tale type: "I was the victim of the Miss Flegg syndrome" (*LO*, p. 149). Miss Flegg is the wicked witch who transforms little Joan into a mothball. The trauma of this experience persists in Terremoto as Joan feels the "Fat Lady" enveloping her: "I gasped for air. Disguised, concealed, white fur choking my nose and mouth" (*LO*, p. 321). But what is Joan? A butterfly disguised as a mothball as she wants to think, or a mothball concealed beneath butterfly wings? When she dances on her balcony at Terremoto with imaginary wings sprouting from her shoulders, she cuts her feet on broken glass — "Some Butterfly." If Joan's reality is uncertain, then how can she be dis-enchanted? Can she ever escape the curse of the "Miss Flegg syndrome"? In fairy tales the answer is categorical; Cinderella is *not* a char-girl. In *Lady Oracle*, as in real life, the answer is ambiguous. Perhaps some hope can be seen for Joan in the fact that she will return to the gray reality of Toronto.

The tale of Bluebeard has specific importance both for *Lady Oracle* and *Stalked by Love*. The parallels between the Bluebeard story and Joan's current Costume Gothic are obvious. In both, the wealthy rapacious male has murdered his previous wives and his present mate faces a similar fate if she enters a forbidden place. The forbidden place is a locked room in the story of Bluebeard and the maze in *Stalked by Love*. When Charlotte enters the maze she is rescued by Redmond (LO, p. 333), but when Felicia ("with red hair and green eyes and small white teeth" so closely resembling her creator) enters the maze, she finds the murdered wives. Redmond is Bluebeard.

Margaret Atwood makes delightful sport of the Bluebeard tale, but Joan is less amused. She identifies with the curious, gullible victim:

> in any labyrinth I would have let go of the thread in order to follow a wandering light, a fleeting voice. In a fairy tale I would be one of the two stupid sisters who open the forbidden door and are shocked by the murdered wives ....[9] (*LO*, p. 152)

Thus, when Felicia/Joan enters the maze — a scene Joan imagines just before the reporter's knock on the door — she finds that the murdered wives are, in fact, her discarded selves, including a fat self in pink tights and skirt with butterfly antennae and "a pair of obviously false wings" (*LO*, p.341). Redmond/Bluebeard is equally diverse:

Cunningly, he began his transformations, trying to lure her into his reach. His face grew a white gauze mask, then a pair of mauve-tinted spectacles, then a red beard and a moustache, which faded, giving place to burning eyes and icicle teeth. Then his cloak vanished and he stood looking at her sadly; he was wearing a turtle-neck sweater.... (*LO*, p. 342)

Bluebeard is a composite of Joan's men, her father, Paul, the Royal Porcupine, the mysterious icicle man from "Lady Oracle," and finally, Arthur. Once again reality and fantasy fuse in Joan's mind with disastrous results.

Armed with Gothic plots and the story of Bluebeard, we can now tackle the maze. As Joan tells us, "Every myth is a version of the truth" (*LO*, p. 92), and in classical myth the maze is closely associated with oracles and rites of rebirth or transformation from one state to another. Mazes (or labyrinths, the terms are interchangeable) were originally intended as tests, either in the tactical defense of a fort or at the entrance to sacred places, especially caves. Their double purpose was either to exclude the undesirable or to provide ingress for the ally or initiate. According to W. F. Jackson Knight, whose work Atwood knows, mazes are key symbols in an ancient matriarchal earth cult involving exclusion from or initiation into new life, or life after death.[10] Mazes guarded the entrance to caves because the cave was the way into Mother Earth, the sacred entrance to death, rebirth, wisdom and descent into the underworld. Knight carries the association of maze, cave, and earth further:

The labyrinth is the boundary between without and within: it is the entrance to the tomb, it is the cave which is the entrance to the earth, and possibly it is the body of the earth mother and of the divine king also.[11]

He goes on to emphasize the links between mazes and the Persephone-Demeter myth as well as the association of prophetic personalities such as Sibyls and Oracles with mazes or caves. Upon reaching the centre of the maze, the initiate finds the desired wisdom or rebirth, often symbolized as a maiden. Properly speaking, then, mazes are not places where the unwary become lost, a popular misconception, but places sacred to the worship and wisdom of Mother Earth.

Without doubt Knight's theories are fascinating, but what possible relation exists between his serious scholarly study and the grizzly maze in *Stalked by Love* or any other part of *Lady Oracle*? Leaving aside "Lady Oracle" herself for the moment, one finds frequent reference to mazes or labyrinths and related concepts in *Lady Oracle*. The Bluebeard stories, for example, are comparable because the forbidden room, one of a long sequence with its special key, is both a test and a tomb. Charlotte thinks of the Redmond Grange maze as a test (*LO*, pp. 331-332), but Joan cannot solve the riddle of the maze herself because she feels that she has "taken a wrong turn somewhere" (*LO*, p. 333). Likewise her experiments with automatic writing are labyrinthine and inconclusive. Entering the mirror is like entering a maze until one evening the candle dies and she is stranded in the long dark corridor "afraid to turn around even" (*LO*, p. 22-23). Metaphorically, of course, Joan's life is a bewildering maze, which meanders "along from one thing to another" (*LO*, p. 7). In addition to her frequent transformations and her longing for new lives, Joan actually undergoes a rite of death and re-birth, surfacing from the waters of Lake Ontario reborn!

The crucial part of any maze is its centre. What or who presides at the centre of Joan's maze? There are at least two possible answers — the Triple Goddess and Joan's selves — and they are connected. Early in her life Joan began to visualize her mother as a monster with three heads and "a curious double mouth" (*LO*, p. 68). This image of the three-headed mother recurs frequently. Joan even sees herself as three-headed when she, like her mother, buys a triple mirror (*LO*, p. 219). Joan's monster-mother is, in fact, her own reflection (*LO*, p. 330), and a type of "rotting albatross":

I dreamed about her often, my three headed mother, menacing and cold. Sometimes she would be sitting in front of her vanity table, sometimes she would be crying. She never laughed or smiled. (*LO*, pp. 213-214)

Not surprisingly, then, when Joan enters the maze of her triple mirror, the woman she discovers there, the "Lady Oracle," is her triple-headed mother ("She is one and three") who, in turn, is a reflection of Joan herself decked out, in the poetry, as the Lady of Shallot (*LO*, p. 226), and a parody of the earth mother:

After a while I could almost see her: she lived under the earth somewhere, or inside something, a cave or a huge building; sometimes she was on a boat. She was enormously powerful,

121

almost like a goddess, but it was an unhappy power. (*LO*, p. 222)

This earth mother, the "Lady Oracle" who is "one and three," recalls Graves' White Goddess, Diana, Venus, Hecate, the three phases of the Moon, and of woman seen in her third role of hag. [12] Joan herself is a mock Persephone who chooses to descend into the maze of her imagination, a Persephone who views her mother as a temptress luring her on (*LO*, p. 330). Furthermore, Joan is the Persephone who must descend into the maze or underworld and be sought for by her mother.

The joke in Atwood's delightful manipulations of maze, goddess, oracle and myth rests in the fact that Joan misses the point entirely; oracles, of course, are often misleading. Not until the end of her story, just prior to her encounter with the hapless reporter, does Joan realize that the woman in the mirror is her mother who is in turn a reflection of Joan herself. And to set her mother free so that she will no longer haunt her, Joan (as Felicia) must enter the maze in *Stalked by Love*. When she does, she discovers the truth:

> *Suddenly she found herself in the central plot. A stone bench ran along one side, and on it were seated four women. Two of them looked a lot like her, with red hair and green eyes and small white teeth. The third was middle-aged, dressed in a strange garment that ended halfway up her calves, with a ratty piece of fur around her neck. The last was enormously fat. She was wearing a pair of pink tights and a short pink skirt covered with spangles.* (*LO*, p. 341)

As the intrepid reader has long suspected, the centre of the maze of *Lady Oracle* is an ornate mirror disguised as a Costume Gothic called *Stalked by Love*. When Joan looks in the mirror (like all good little Brownies, (*LO*, p. 61), she sees herself — as fat girl, as Louisa K. Delacourt writer of romances, as Joan Foster wife, and as Joan Foster poetess and "culture heroine." What Joan learns is that she irrevocably contains these four selves, she is "one and three," and that "every man has more than one wife. Sometimes all at once, sometimes one at a time, sometimes ones he doesn't even know about" (*LO*, p. 341). Thus, Atwood supplies a fresh interpretation of the Bluebeard story: women are not curious by nature, but multiple.

To what end has Atwood created this ornate, elaborate structure in which mythology, Gothic romance, and fairy tale play an interlocking role? In part she creates the maze of *Lady Oracle* for the sheer joy of creation — and reading. This maze, however, is both more and less than it seems — more complicated, as we have seen, and less serious. Atwood's mixture of comedy, satire and parody does not allow soul-searching interpretations.

The humour lies both in the fantastic situations of Joan's life, whether as fat child dressed in a butterfly costume or as desperate "culture heroine" confronting an interviewer, and in the verbal wit of her narration. Joan is a master at self-caricature; she has learned Miss Flegg's lesson well. Thus, when she remembers herself tied in the ravine for the bad man she admits, "I can't have been a very exciting sexual object, a fat, snotty-nosed eight-year-old in a Brownie outfit" (*LO*, pp. 62-63). Although Joan's witticisms are largely unconscious, Atwood's are not; therefore, the code that Joan and Sam arrange to signal the outcome of Joan's drowning sounds like a satiric jab worthy of the "Royal Canadian Air Farce":

> I tore it [Sam's communiqué] open and read a single word: BETHUNE. That was the code word for success. If there had been a fiasco, the letter would have said TRUDEAU.
> (*LO*, p. 185)

The satire proper in *Lady Oracle*, though equally laconic, is more cutting. Everything from the snobbery of Toronto suburbs, nationalist fervor and empty rhetoric (*Resurgence*), to charlatans peddling spiritualism and Canadian publishing (Black Widow Press/Anansi, Morton and Sturgess/McClelland and Stewart), is fair game. Atwood pokes fun at traditions in Canadian writing including her own:

> Why in *Lady Oracle* is the con-create artist's form squashed animals? It's a direct reference to my own book of criticism as well as the whole tradition of Canadian animal stories. In Italy the animals come in rococco poses.... But for Canada they have to be squashed and frozen.[13]

In fact, Atwood satirizes many aspects of her own writing as well as of her public image: Joan, the poetess, is a "culture heroine" adored by some, accused of being a "ball-stomper" by others. Even her death becomes a cult which she cannot repudiate by coming back to life: "Women scorned to the contrary," Joan realizes, "nothing matched the fury of a deceived death cultist" (*LO*, p. 314). The quantities of food (shades of *The Edible Woman*), the power struggles between Joan and her men, even the mock drowning and surfacing are tongue-in-check jibes at so-called Atwood obsessions. Lake Ontario, after all, is no cool Northern lake "blue as redemption," and Joan's dive is a fraud from start to smelly finish. Even the voluptuous Felicia, her creator's double, is an Atwood victim for, as Atwood points out in *Survival*, there are no Venuses in Canadian literature.

In addition to providing humour and satire, *Lady Oracle* is a sustained double parody of the realist novel on one hand and of the Gothic romance on the other. Indeed, the irony of the novel lies in the fact that it is a *double* parody. *Lady Oracle* shares much with Austen's *Northanger Abbey*, itself a deliberate parody of the popular Gothics of the time. Like Catherine Moreland, Joan scarcely seems "born to be an heroine." In order to rectify this situation Joan and Catherine are fed generous doses of appropriate "phaff." For Catherine this comprises tender snippets from Gray and Thompson. For the 20th century Joan, maudlin melodramatic movies suffice. But Joan's life acquires proportions quite beyond those of the humble Catherine's. Joan flees to Italy, the country, *par excellence*, of Gothic adventure and her 'end' is ambiguous.

Perhaps more important is the difference in narrative voice between *Lady Oracle* and *Northanger Abbey*. Jane Austen's narrator never leaves us in any doubt as to her, and our, ironic distance from the naive Catherine. We are invited to laugh, with the narrator, at Catherine's foolish confusions of Gothicism and real life. The irony in *Lady Oracle* is far more subtle because there is no ironic gap between the narrator and her tale; Joan tells her own story.

First person narration is a common convention in 20th century realist fiction, but despite the truthfulness implied by this convention, we have more reason to suspect Joan than to believe her. *Lady Oracle* uses and mocks other realist conventions as well: for example, we are able to read the novel the narrator is *actually* writing, people and places are recreated with convincing detail, and Joan provides an etiology for her behaviour by way of chronological explanation of her life. We are being asked to believe that this preposterous story really happened. Yet, as Joan frequently points out, her life reads like a Gothic romance plot: "This was the reason I fabricated my life, time after time: the truth was not convincing" (*LO*, p. 150).

Joan Foster, alias Louisa K. Delacourt, is a thoroughly Quixotic heroine, "hooked on plots," and unable to maintain clear distinctions between reality and fantasy. Her biography, therefore, sounds like an imitation of her own fiction. Although Joan learns very little, the reader is able to perceive the irony of Joan's position because that irony exists in the gap between our expectations of realist fiction and Joan's absurd 'autobiography,' and in the *absence* of a gap between Joan's life and her Costume Gothics. By imperceptible stages Joan's realist narrative approaches her Costume Gothic, *Stalked by Love*, until the latter absorbs the former. *Stalked by Love* becomes a parody of Joan's life and vice versa. In the absence of a more traditional ironic distance between narrator and story, this double parody provides the lens, or two-way mirror, through which we are able to see and judge Joan.

The irony, and with it much of the satire and humour in *Lady Oracle*, is a function of the duplistic structure of the narrative — novel reflects Gothic, Gothic reflects Joan's life. There is even a hint of a further ironic doubling in the pages of "Lady Oracle"; Joan is apprehensive because the poetry closely resembles her Costume Gothics "gone wrong" (*LO*, p. 232), and Arthur is angry because the poetry apparently reflects their marriage. The treatment of duality in *Lady Oracle*, while amusing, is more than an object of satire or the subject of "funhouse-mirror reflection" (*LO*, p. 251). Atwood has once again explored the duplicity of life on several levels.

Under the pressures of reality the individual seeks escape in a world of fantasy where adventure and danger resolve themselves into simple categories and all conclusions are happy. It is because Joan so deeply feels reality that she must continue to write her Gothics; they are a means of escape:

> As long as I could spend a certain amount of time each week as Louisa, I was all right.... But if I was cut off, if I couldn't work at my current Costume Gothic, I would become mean and irritable, drink too much and start to cry. (*LO*, p. 213)

When the Royal Porcupine enters her life, her Gothics are no longer necessary. But when he transforms himself back into Chuck Brewer by murdering his fantastic self, she leaves:

> For him, reality and fantasy were the same thing, which meant that for him there was no reality. But for me it would mean there was no fantasy, and therefore no escape. (*LO*, p. 270)

125

The need for a fantasy life in the midst of obdurate reality is innocuous enough. Only when the individual becomes confused between reality and fantasy, between life and art, do the problems commence. Throughout her life Joan struggles to plot events, achieve happy endings, and typecast her friends. Thus, her men must be heroes or villains and when they reveal themselves as gray and complicated instead of good or bad, she tries to discard them. Equally damaging is her treatment of herself. Because she longs to be a heroine in a romantic scenario, she tries to discard those parts of herself that do not fit the role: "I... was a sorry assemblage of lies and alibis, each complete in itself but rendering the others worthless" (*LO*, p. 211). The tangle she creates becomes so convoluted that she plots drastic measures, but her metaphorical death cuts her off, in reality, leaving her stranded in Terremoto with family and friends "on the other side."

When reality catches up with Joan in the shape of Sam's lawyer and a newspaper reporter, the lesson it teaches is that Joan must accept her own duplicity, in both senses of the word. In telling her story, she realizes that: "I was more than double, I was triple, multiple..." (*LO*, p. 246). There are, in fact, five Joans — Joan Delacourt the fat girl, Joan Foster the thin, beautiful wife, Louisa K. Delacourt, Joan the cult figure, and Joan the narrator of *Lady Oracle* who contains the other Joans. The chief split, however, from which the other selves arise, is between a prosaic, gray, complicated Joan and a Joan of gothic extremes. She realizes that others are double as well and cannot be confined within her romantic pigeon-holes:

Every man I'd ever been involved with, I realized, had had two selves: my father, healer and killer; the man in the tweed coat, my rescuer and possibly also a pervert; the Royal Porcupine and his double, Chuck Brewer; even Paul.... (*LO*, p. 292)

Arthur, she admits, has as many selves as she does, although she is simultaneous and he is a sequence (*LO*, p. 211).

What *Lady Oracle* implies is not that duplicity is either immoral or inaccurate, but that we are all double, perhaps multiple. This condition becomes immoral or psychologically untenable when the desire to be one is reduced to the need to be "single-minded, single-hearted, single-bodied" (*LO*, p. 211). The oracle tells us that she is "one and three," a multiplicity with unity. It is learning how to live, practically, with this knowledge that is difficult.

Atwood, understandably, does not take her heroine back to

reality. To do so would turn her novel into a tract. There are, therefore, several questions that complicate the conclusion of *Lady Oracle*. To what degree is Joan alone responsible for her messy life or to what degree is she a victim of her social-climbing, unhappy mother, of Miss Flegg, Hollywood stereotypes and so on? Are her caustic portraits of others, especially Arthur, valid? If so, one wonders, how did a beautiful, talented woman like Joan become involved with such a vapid "loser"? Does Joan realize the damage she has caused, and is her resolution to return to Toronto and to give up Costume Gothics for science fiction sufficient redress? In fact, Joan's decision to return is a definite gamble, for there is no guarantee that she will be forgiven, believed, or accepted for what she is. If we are to believe the scenario in the last episode from *Stalked by Love*, returning to Toronto is the worst step possible:

"How did you get here?" Felicia asked. "Why can't you go back to the outside world?"
"Back?" said the first woman. "We have all tried to go back. That was our mistake." (*LO*, p. 342)

Presumably, this threat is simply a figment of Joan's Gothic imagination and no irony is meant to reflect upon the end of her narrative.

To some extent, the questions hovering over the conclusion of *Lady Oracle* are deliberate on Atwood's part. The novelist who provides answers to his questions soon finds he is not writing a novel. There is, however, a larger ambiguity, or inconclusiveness, in *Lady Oracle* that may not be as conscious. As with *The Edible Woman*, it is the irony of first person narration in *Lady Oracle* that is suspect. Despite the fun and wit, Atwood does make a serious comment upon life; fat Joan is cruelly treated and, in turn, casually if not vindictively, abuses others. And yet there is no way for the reader to be certain that anything has changed by the end of Joan's narration. Quite possibly she will begin to spin another plot, this time around the new man in her life. The moral dilemma raised by Joan's story — liberty versus responsibility — is not faced squarely. Instead Joan (if not Atwood) throws us a casual remark — "I don't think I'll ever be a very tidy person" — and eludes our grasp.

Atwood has said that her heroine makes a very small advance:

Before she said I will hide who I am because nobody will like who I am. They will not accept me, They will think I'm ridiculous. If I can conceal myself, then I will be safe. So she's gotten as far as saying I am who I am, take it or leave it ....[14]

Joan has said that she is an escape artist, and the thought does not depress her:

> I might as well face it, I thought, I was an artist, an escape artist.... the real romance of my life was that between Houdini and his ropes and locked trunk; entering the embrace of bondage, slithering out again. What else had I ever done?
>
> (*LO*, p. 334)

Whether Joan's story is another Miss Flegg manoeuvre or not, she does appear to have heeded her oracle. She has entered the maze and found new life. For Joan, rebirth consists in accepting her selves. Instead of spreading "like crabgrass... fire... cancer or public lice" (*LO*, p. 319), as does Felicia, her Gothic double, she must learn to "contain" her selves. The wisdom of the oracle is simple enough — to thine own selves be true.

Lady Oracle can be read on several different levels. It as an amusing parody of Gothic romance and realist conventions, a satiric commentary upon Atwood's own experiences as a writer and upon aspects of contemporary society, and a portrayal of "the perils of Gothic thinking." While it may not offer answers or entirely satisfying resolutions (what oracle does?), it raises some serious enough questions. But the real delight, for the reader, lies in exploring the complicated maze of humour, satire and parody that is Lady Oracle.

Chapter VIII

Choosing Violent Duality

> This country is something that must be chosen — it is so
> easy to leave — and if we choose it we are still choosing a
> violent duality. (*JSM*, p. 62)

Attempting to place Margaret Atwood in a broad context is, as I
pointed out at the beginning, difficult and explorative. An obvious
complication is her age. She is just forty and, if she continues to be
as creative as she has already been, we can expect new developments
in her art. At present she has established herself as a major Canadian writer, but she is rapidly acquiring an international stature as
well; she is read and taught abroad, particularly in England and the
United States, and her fiction shares much with that of foreign con-
temporaries. Although it may be precipitous to assess her importance or evaluate her work, a few observations can be made which
will provide some perspective on her writing, thereby com-
plementing the textual analyses of preceding chapters. If my
speculations about her tradition or my evaluations prove wrong,
this should not invalidate the readings of individual texts.

Margaret Atwood has remarked that her poetic tradition is
Canadian; she "learned to write from people in this country." [1] Her
affinity with D. C. Scott's world of contrasts and F. R. Scott's satire
is apparent in theme and style. Both Scotts achieved marked success
with the brief cut-off line which Atwood uses to such effect in her
poetry. Her nearest of kin, however, are James Reaney and, possibly, Jay Macpherson. Atwood knows both writers well and worked
closely with them during her formative years, 1959-1965, when she
published poetry, reviews and criticisms in *Alphabet*. [2]

Influenced by Frye, both Reaney and Macpherson believe in the
power of the imagination to create autonomous poetic worlds.
Atwood, while celebrating the imagination, often in disturbing
images that recall, for example, Reaney's *The Red Heart* (1949) or
Macpherson's *Welcoming Disaster* (1974), is aware of its dangers.
In her poetry physical reality constantly assails imagination, challenging its proud autonomy so that the poet must adopt an ironic eye

129

and an ambivalent attitude towards both realms. Atwood further resembles Reaney in the emphasis she places upon perception, although she is again less willing than he to trust the eye of the beholder, the individual's inner vision. Her use of myth owes much to Reaney's theories in *Alphabet*, as noted in the discussion of *The Journals of Susanna Moodie* in Chapter III, because Reaney provided a model for the intersection of immediate experience and myth. Macpherson's *The Boatman*, published in 1957, was one of Canada's first series of poems artistically shaped as a book instead of a collection. With *Double Persephone, The Circle Game, The Journals of Susanna Moodie*, and to a lesser degree in other volumes, Atwood creates comparable unity — poems inter-related through theme and image to create a structural and imaginative whole.

Atwood's differences from Reaney and Macpherson underline her affinities with poets like Al Purdy and Dennis Lee. Both write about personal experience and historical event in a style that relies less on myth, symbol, or imaginative structure than on colloquial speech rhythms and statement. Though fascinated by the power of imagination and the independence of a verbal universe, Atwood remains committed to social and ethical perspectives in her art. As well, her style is one of direct personal address or dramatic monologue which involves a deft use of colloquialisms; even the most ordinary words, "this" or "but", carry startling importance. Because the theory of art as mirror or map, outlined in *Survival*, is basic to her writing, one should admire the beauty of the mirror, the colour and complexity of the map, without neglecting the social relevance of poem or novel, the connection between art and life.

This connection indicates the central dialectic and tension in Atwood's work, the pull towards art on one hand and towards life on the other. How does one capture living forms in imaginative and verbal structures? How does the artist work from life to art and still reflect life? Atwood asks these questions repeatedly, from the two immortalities of *Double Persephone*, the opposing countries of *The Animals in That Country* and Moodie's double voice, the conflicting perceptions of objective reality in *The Circle Game* and *Power Politics*, to Circe's fear of "the story" in *You Are Happy*. The tension that exists between art and life informs the subject/object dialectic as well. Atwood's artistic world rests upon a Blakean world of contraries and William Blake is, I suspect, the most significant non-Canadian influence upon Atwood's imagination. Blake's influence, however, may not be either direct or overt, for he lies behind both Reaney and Macpherson and was, of course, the subject of

Frye's *Fearful Symmetry* (1947). Blake, as it were, was in the Toronto air of the '50's.

More important than Atwood's relationship to other poets is the development of her own voice and style. While a cool, acerbic wit, ironic eye and laconic phrase are characteristic of her poetry, she continues to explore new forms. Up to and including *You Are Happy*, the combination of detachment and irony coupled with cut-off line and duplistic form dominates her poetry. *Selected Poems* marks a plateau in this development.

The latest volume, *Two Headed Poems*, contains a greater variety of form, voice and theme indicating, perhaps, new directions.[3] There are, for example, some excellent poems about early settlers, "Four Small Elegies," and several sensuous lyrics describing the days or seasons, as in "Daybooks I, # 7":

> November, the empty month; we try
> to fill it with the smells
> of cooking earth: baked roots, the comfort
> of windfall pears, potatoes
> flowry and round,... (*THP*, p. 32)

In several poems Atwood presents the contrast and gap between private contentment and public dread; domestic security and importance collapses in the larger context of politics and war. This universal human irony, presented so forcefully in "Solstice Poem," is a version of our "two-headed" existence and the thematic centre of the collection. She also explores the relationships among grandmothers, mothers and daughters, capturing a fresh and intimate awareness of the generations. The most striking feature of these poems is the creation of various different presences. In addition to the private voice of the earlier poetry, we hear the voices of mother, grandmother, floorsweeper, prisoner and two nations. There is less immediate, private anger in these poems and a strong mood of reflection, almost musing, upon past and future. Atwood emerges here with a gentler, more mellow, wisdom.

As a fiction writer Atwood's tradition is tenuous. Her novels are best read in the context of twentieth-century fiction where first person narrators, ironic self-reflexive narratives, and symbolic or even mythic structures, are common. There are, however, elements that place her within a broadly-defined Canadian tradition: Atwood's emphasis on the past and the individual's need to be part of a social context, as well as her treatment of victimization and struggle for survival, are common features in our novels. In *The Edible Woman* and *Lady Oracle*, Atwood consciously draws upon the tradition of Canadian satire from Haliburton to Leacock and Davies. This satire is heavily ironic and self-critical, while affirming fundamental human values — Marion, for example, is not a Yahoo, nor is Joan a Billy Pilgrim or an Oedipa Maas.

Although Atwood's published fiction is polished and enjoyable, it is as a poet that she is truly distinctive and commanding. There are several reasons for this distinction between the power of her poetry and prose. Some of these are matters of voice and style. The sense of challenge and tension so effective in the poems is harder to maintain in a narrative. Moreover, the ironic exploration of self, a constant Atwood theme, is more successful in the poems because the irony of first person narration in the novels too often blurs. The poems are more dramatic vehicles for the exploration of the self because of the possibilities they provide for abrupt juxtaposition of points of view or creation of hallucinatory distortions of a solipsistic eye. With the exception of *Surfacing*, Atwood fails to sustain in her fiction the eerie, disembodied voice that rivets our attention in the poetry. Beckett's experiments with voice in *Molloy*, *Malone Dies*, and *The Unnameable* resemble the voice in Atwood's poetry, but in general the novel form cannot avoid some sense of ego, of particularized individuality. Certainly, it is in her poetry that Atwood best combines voice and style in order to explore perception, the philosophical extremes of solipsist and materialist, and her concept of the self as a place where experiences intersect.

The closest Atwood comes to resolving the paradoxes of self and perception is in terms of duplicity. Duality is neither negative nor ambivalent. Duality, whether of structure or metaphor, is not the same as polarity. But the human tendency to polarize experience, to affirm one perspective while denying the other, is deeply ingrained, and this makes choosing to live with duality very difficult. The difficulty of this choice, again a major theme in the new collection, emphasizes the continuity between *Two-Headed Poems* and the other books.

Companion poems from *Two-Headed Poems* present duplicity directly and amusingly. In the first, "The Woman Who Could Not Live with her Faulty Heart," the speaker complains:

But most hearts say, I want, I want,
I want, I want. My heart
is more duplicitous,

though no twin as I once thought.
It says, I want, I don't want, I
want, and then a pause.
It forces me to listen, (*THP*, p. 15)

Beginning with the fact of physiological doubling, Atwood develops the idea into a hostile polarization; the woman and her "duplicitous" heart are at odds instead of being comfortable duplicates. In "The Woman Makes Peace with her Faulty Heart," she proclaims an "uneasy truce":

But you've shoved me this far
old pump, and we're hooked
together like conspirators, which
we are, and just as distrustful. (*THP*, p. 87)

While this truce is certainly no state of productive harmony, it does indicate a sardonic acceptance of duplicity; they need each other after all, these two, and together they work.

In "Marrying the Hangman," a prose poem, and one of the finest in the new volume, Atwood returns to problems of perceptual and sexual polarity first explored in *Double Persephone* and continued in *The Circle Game*, *Power Politics* and *You Are Happy*. The condemned woman can only save her life by marrying the hangman — a legal option in 18th century Quebec. But this time, unlike the union in "Book of Ancestors" (*YAH*), there is no affirmation because in saving her life, she also loses it; she exchanges "one locked room for another" and remains trapped in a world without mirrors, her function being to reflect favourably on her new husband.

Atwood portrays the contemporary national dilemma, Quebec separatism, in terms of violent duality in one of her most challenging poems from the new collection, the title sequence "Two-Headed Poems." Duality is a fact of our national character. Canadian history has always involved an "uneasy truce" which now threatens to polarize the country. As one moves through the eleven sections of this poem, two voices, one French the other English Canadian, squabble and complain about each other's customs, stereotypes, and their shared history. "Our leader" reflects this duality with his two voices, heads, etc., but he is accepted and trusted by neither group: "how can you use two languages / and mean what you say in both?" At times the voices overlap, ironically speaking as one without realizing it. This accusation, for example, is flung from neither side,

133

and yet from each simultaneously:

> You want the air
> but not the words that come with it:
> breathe at your peril. (*THP*, p. 71)

Language is the chief source of contention. Each ethnic group has two dreams, one of linguistic freedom —

> a song
> which rises liquid and effortless,
> our double, gliding beside us
> over all these rivers, borders, (*THP*, p. 75)

and the other — "to be mute." These dreams are futile, however, because they represent extreme opposites, absolute victory or defeat for one side or the other. Resolution is impossible where there is no communication. The double voice concludes that,

> This is not a debate
> but a duet
> with two deaf singers. (*THP*, p. 75)

The possibility of affirmation through "choosing a violent duality" which informs *The Journals of Susanna Moodie*, which Moodie herself symbolizes, is not heard in "Two-Headed Poems" for the singers are deaf.

If A. J. M. Smith was correct in his 1962 Introduction to *Masks of Poetry*, then duality, or as he calls it "a dichotomy," characterizes our literature. This much, at least, is clear: Atwood shares her interest in duality and her vision of affirmation through duality with writers like Robertson Davies and Sheila Watson while others, such as Robert Kroetsch, struggle less hopefully with the concept.

For Atwood the dynamic of violent duality is a function of the creative act. From *Double Persephone*, to *Lady Oracle* and now *Two Headed-Poems*, she has continued to explore the inescapable tension between art and life, the two immortalities — "One of earth lake trees," the other of "Hard marble, carven word" (*DP*). She is constantly aware of opposites — self/other, subject/object, male/female, nature/man — and of the need to accept and work within them. To create, Atwood chooses violent dualities, and her art re-works, probes, and dramatizes the ability to see double.

Postscript

Life Before Man

(1979)

Since the time of writing this introduction to Margaret Atwood's work, she has published not only *Two-Headed Poems* but also her fourth novel, *Life Before Man*.[1] What follows here are some preliminary thoughts on the new novel and its relation to Atwood's preceding work. I am prompted to offer these thoughts, tentative as they are, firstly in the effort to make this study as comprehensive as possible, and secondly because I suspect that, together with *Two-Headed Poems*, *Life Before Man* marks the beginning of what may prove to be a new stage in Atwood's artistic evolution.

Life Before Man is Atwood's first attempt at social and domestic realism. The novel covers two years in the lives of three ordinary people — Elizabeth and her husband Nate, and Nate's new lover, Lesje, for whom he leaves his wife — charting the development and deterioration of their relationships within the context of daily routine, miscommunication, tawdry affairs and gray emotional struggles. There are other, peripheral characters such as Chris, who has shot himself before the narrative begins, Martha now discarded by Nate for the apparently more sensitive Lesje, Lesje's boyfriend William, and a number of relatives. Although the secondary characters provide something of a particularizing context for the three main characters — through Elizabeth's tyrannical Aunt Muriel, for example, we receive something of an etiology for Elizabeth's repression and selfishness – Elizabeth, Nate and Lesje are more alike than different. Their responses to life, their indecisiveness and triviality, envelop them like a gray blanket. Of course, this gray sameness can be a legitimate result of realist fiction. And seen against the claustrophobia of Toronto and the Royal Ontario Museum, these lives mirror the monotony and emptiness surrounding them.

Atwood presents her characters from the outside through a limited, third person narrative that shifts point of view from Elizabeth to Nate to Lesje, in turn, as they go through the motions of daily existence. This is the first time since *The Edible Woman* that Atwood has used third person narrative, and the first time she has used it to suggest three separate points of view, one of them male. While Atwood handles point of view skilfully, especially at the beginning to create a sympathetic picture of Nate, the very necessity for separate points of view is ironically undercut by the boring sameness of these people. Furthermore, with the partial exception of Lesje, their inner lives are as devoid of drama or interest as their outer lives. Lesje at least has a fantasy life. In a manner reminiscent of Lucy Swithin from Virginia Wolf's *Between the Acts*, she wanders in pre-history, imagining herself as a "tourist or refugee," observing the stegosaurs and camptosaurs in their Jurassic swamps.[2] She can indulge in these fantasies — regressive ones she knows — because she is something of a paleontology expert herself. Only in these fantasies can she both escape the present world of men and re-create a dinosaur world unlike the one she is employed to construct in the museum: "She mixes eras, adds colors: why not a metallic blue Stegosaurus with red and yellow dots instead of the dull greys and browns postulated by the experts?... Only when the camptosaurs are dead do they turn grey" (*LBM*, p. 19).

Supporting the shifting point of view in the novel is the linear, temporal organization provided by specific dates that progress from "Friday, October 29, 1976" to "Friday, August 18, 1978." With the exception of two dated flashbacks to earlier moments in the characters' lives, the dates march steadily forward like diary entries or the pages of a calendar, and together with point of view, these dates provide the only structure in the novel. Clearly, Atwood is examining the juxtaposition of inner time (memory, subjective sense of duration) with outer, public time as measured by history. Public events, however, seem to have as little significance or purpose as the lives of these people. Like the War Measures Act in 1970, Remembrance Day, the November 15, 1976 election of the *Parti Québécois* or Lesje's February 16, 1977 scene with William, events merely hapen without logic or continuity, leaving the precise, self-important dates to comment ironically upon vacuity of private and public contemporary life.

In *Life Before Man*, Atwood has dropped the romance conventions of her previous novels — the fantasy and satire of *The Edible Woman*, the mythic force of *Surfacing* and the Gothic ironies of *Lady Oracle* — in order to capture the empty inconclusiveness of modern marriage and urban existence. She does so with remarkable success, but unfortunately, the subject is one that is already overexploited and more tedious than terrifying. Something else is needed to carry this realist subject when convolutions of plot or the symbolic power of language cannot be used. Technically, *Life Before Man* is much like Faulkner's *The Sound and the Fury* or Lowry's *Under the Volcano*, narratives that tell their stories of contemporary decay through shifting point of view. But these comparisons, I feel, reveal deficiencies in *Life Before Man*, for Atwood's language and characters lack the depth and passion of either Faulkner's or Lowry's.

Elizabeth is the only character whose repression and anger are disturbing, the only one whose past losses and traumas seem at all commensurate with her present negativity. After she passes out, to her amazement, at Aunt Muriel's funeral, she ponders her lover's suicide and the surfaces and depths of her life:

> How close has she come, how many times, to doing what Chris did? More important: what stopped her?...
> But she's still alive, she wears clothes, she walks around, she holds down a job even. She has two children. Despite the rushing of wind, the summoning voices she can hear from underground, the dissolving trees, the chasms that open at her feet; and will always from time to time open.... (*LBM*, pp. 301-302)

The most alarming aspect of Elizabeth's life, however, is not her recognition of chasms, but her inertia and her final sense that life consists of surface realities and that ideals are lies. Like the speaker in Beckett's *The Unnameable*, she will merely "go on."

Despite differences in style and narrative strategy between the

137

other novels and *Life Before Man*, this novel should not be un-familiar because its realistic world is as much a constant in Atwood's fiction as her satire or gothicisms. This is what Joan Foster's world would look like if viewed from the outside. This is the world that Marion McAlpin narrowly and temporarily avoids. More importantly, this is the world that the narrator of *Surfacing* leaves behind her in the city, and it is the world to which she will most likely return. Why has Atwood chosen to confront this gray urban emptiness head on in *Life Before Man*? One answer lies in the possibility that *Life Before Man* relates to the earlier fiction much as *Two-Headed Poems* relates to the earlier poetry. In both works Atwood explores new subjects and techniques in the effort to re-evaluate and expand her earlier vision. That vision, characterized by its "violent duality," its cataclysms ("I judge you as the trees do by dying," *PP*, p. 33), its magic and transformations, is giving way to a much more subtle, mellow, even pessimistic vision, undistanced from reality by irony and laconic wit, unmediated by metaphor and fantasy. Thus, the subjects in *Two-Headed Poems*, as in *Life Before Man*, are not those of myth, power politics and gothic extremes, but grand-mothers, history, children, neighbours and daily routine.

The power of art itself continues to be questioned (and in a more radical way) in Atwood's latest work, whether that art is poetic metaphor or romance convention. In "Five Poems for Grand-mothers," for example, the poet confesses that art is powerless against the nebulous inconclusiveness of daily experience; art is a charm made "from nothing but paper; which is good/ for exactly nothing" (*THP*, p. 39). In *Life Before Man*, the artist withdraws behind realist conventions, appearing only as the hand that chooses a title, the self-important dates that head each section, and the prefac-ing quotes. Through these selected glimpses of her presence, Atwood implies not only that we are trapped in our mundanity, but that history, science and art cannot redeem us, offer alternatives, or even shape the dull routine of our lives. *Life Before Man* has a final page, but no conclusion, no finality, no *anagnorisis*. Elizabeth, Nate and Lesje will simply go on, unable to feel and unaware that they are already museum pieces, gray dinosaurs. The lesson from pre-history is that history repeats itself, and "what defeats us, as always, is/ the repetition" (*THP*, p. 24).

Notes

Chapter I

[1] *Survival: A Thematic Guide to Canadian Literature* (Toronto: Anansi, 1972), p. 13. All further references are to this edition.

[2] "Interview with Margaret Atwood," Linda Sandler, *The Malahat Review*, 41 (January, 1977), p. 17.

Chapter II

[1] I have not attempted to discuss all of Atwood's early poetry, published or unpublished, because I am not primarily interested in tracing evolution in theme or technique in poems that have little to recommend them except that they were written by the young Atwood. I discuss selected examples from among the early published poems that have literary merit and assist clarification of a given point.

[2] These six chapbooks consist of *Double Persephone* (1961), see note #4 below, *The Circle Game* (1964) consisting of the title poem from the later volume, *Talismans for Children* (1965), *Kaleidescopes: Baroque* (1965), *Speeches for Doctor Frankenstein* (1966) and *Expeditions* (1966). All were published in limited editions.

[3] "The Seven Wonders," *The Canadian Forum*, 40 (August, 1960), 114-115; "Avalon Revisited," *Fiddlehead*, 55 (Winter, 1963), 10-13.

[4] *Double Persephone* (Toronto: Hawkshead Press, 1961), p. 4. A limited edition of two hundred copies was printed. Atwood typeset and prepared the striking linocut cover illustration herself.

[5] Frank Davey has made an excellent study of stasis in Atwood's

poetry, beginning with *Double Persephone*. He focuses his argument upon the polarity of time and space as a way of describing form, image, and theme. See "Atwood's Gorgon Touch," *Studies in Canadian Literature* (Summer, 1977), 146-163.

[6] "The Witch & the Nightingale," and "The Whore & the Dove *Alphabet* (December, 1962), 44-45, 48-49, were published as fables and accompanied by drawings by Harold Town. Fables and drawings were a regular feature of *Alphabet*.

[7] "Poor Tom," *Alphabet*, 6 (June, 1963), 52. The four poems printed in this issue are "The Orphan From Alberta," "Poor Tom," "Mad Mother Ballad" and "Little Nell," pages 51-54.

[8] "Fall and All: A Sequence" appeared in *Fiddlehead*, 59 (Winter, 1964), 58-63. There are eight poems: "Fall and All," "The Revenant," "The Acid Sibyl," "The Siamese Twins," "The Revelation," "The Double Nun," and "The Witch's House." "Talismans" and "Kaleidescopes" were published individually; see #2 above.

[9] George Bowering, *Al Purdy* (Toronto: Copp Clark, 1970).

[10] Interview, *Eleven Canadian Novelists* by Graeme Gibson (Toronto: Anansi, 1973), p. 6. Subsequent references are indicated as Gibson, followed by the page number.

[11] The repetition of "I want" seems to embody an affirmation of commitment to life, a dropping of defences and masks that insulate the speaker. For example, in "A Pursuit" from *The Animals in That Country*:

> I want you
> to be
> a place for me
> to search in
>
> I want you to be
> there
> to be
> found. (*AC*, p. 67)

And again in "There is Only One of Everything" from *You Are Happy*:

> *I can even say it,*
> *though only once and it won't*

last: *I want this. I want*
this. (*YAH*, p. 92)

[12] T. S. Eliot, *Collected Poems* (London; Faber & Faber Ltd., 1963), p. 78.

[13] Earle Birney, "Bushed" in *Poetry of Mid-Century 1940-1960* (Toronto: McClelland & Stewart, 1964), p. 34.

Chapter III

[1] Susanna (Strickland) Moodie (1803-1885), an English gentlewoman and wife of Major James Moodie, emigrated in 1832 and spent her first eight years in the bush near the Otonabee River. After her husband's contribution to the suppression of the 1837 Rebellion, the Moodies moved to relative comfort in Belleville. She died in Toronto. Susanna Moodie is mentioned in works such as *The Oxford Companion of Canadian History and Literature*, and excerpts from her works are anthologized in Canadian literature surveys. *Roughing it in the Bush* has been re-issued in McClelland and Stewart's NCL series. For a thorough bio-bibliographical reference, see Alec Lucas, *The Otonabee School* (Montreal: Mansfield Book Mart Ltd., 1977), 8-9.

[2] In her interesting study of Atwood, Carolyn Allen suggests that Moodie has really failed because she does not realize her desire for "complete transformations." I think, however, that Atwood is more concerned with the transformation of English gentlewoman into Canadian, and history into myth; on both accounts the transformation is dramatically complete. Moodie is not trying to resolve doubleness, but to accept and work with it. See Allen's "Margaret Atwood: Power of Transformation, Power of Knowledge," *Essays on Canadian Writing*, 6 (Spring, 1977), p. 10.

[3] Atwood entitles some of her poems after Moodie's stories as, for example, "Brian the Still-Hunter" and "The Charivari," both from *Roughing it in the Bush*. Her play *Grace Marks*, televised as *The Servant Girl*, CBC, January, 1974, is based upon chapter X of Moodie's *Life in the Clearings*.

⁴ Atwood discusses the predominance of Hecate or Crone figures in Canadian literature in *Survival*, Chapter X. Referring to Graves' concept of three categories, Diana or Maiden figure, Venus, and Hecate or Crone, Atwood remarks that there are few Canadian Venuses. Certainly, Mrs. Moodie is no Venus. It is better, therefore, to speak of her as the classical Triple Goddess figure Diana/Luna/Hecate who is associated with the moon in each of her roles.

⁵ Each of the nineteen issues of *Alphabet*, edited by Reaney from 1960-1971 and "Devoted to the Iconography of the Imagination," contained a "juxtaposition" of myth and documentary. A classical myth, Narcissus or such, would be discussed; contemporary poetry or fiction would follow using the same myth. Of the Dionysus myth Reaney said: "The Story of Dionysus is every child's story only heightened ..." *Alphabet*, 2 (July, 1961), Editorial. In his Editorial for *Alphabet*, 6 (June, 1963), he explained that the myth of Job is documented in the Donnellys.

⁶ James Reaney, "The Canadian Poet's Predicament," in *Masks of Poetry*, ed. A. J. M. Smith (Toronto: McClelland & Stewart, 1962), p. 111.

⁷ While it may be possible to argue that Reaney has developed along similar lines, the dominant impression is that he begins, as does Northrop Frye, with archetypes and moves from these to life, rather than vice versa.

⁸ Taken from an unpublished interview with Sheila Watson at McGill University in May, 1976.

⁹ F. R. Scott, "Laurentian Shield," in *Poets Between the Wars*, ed. Milton Wilson (Toronto: McClelland & Stewart, 1969), p. 91.

¹⁰ A. M. Klein, "Portrait of the Poet as Landscape," in *Poets Between the Wars*, pp. 193-194.

Chapter IV

¹ The cover design for *Power Politics* (Toronto: Anansi, 1972) is by William Kimber, presumably with Atwood's approval. The figure of the Hanged Man is the twelfth arcunum and he embodies sacrifice on all levels. As the archetype, he is Christ: as human being, he is the

individual whose inner harmony serves the community (*caritas*); as nature, he is the sun whose energy gives life. The hanged figure symbolizes the violent death associated with the card. Interpretations vary in details, but see, for example, Mouni Sadhu, *The Tarot* (London: Allen & Unwin, Ltd., 1962).

² This remark comes from "The Twist of Feeling" for the CBC program *Ideas* (November, 1971) in which she discussed *PP*; readings were by Gwen Thomas.

³ CBC *Ideas* (November, 1971).

⁴ George Woodcock calls these poems examples of Atwood's "skill at the poetic booby trap." "Margaret Atwood: Poet as Novelist" in *The Canadian Novelist in the Twentieth Century* (Toronto: McClelland & Stewart Ltd., 1975), p. 312.

⁵ Atwood referred to the poem as a "newsreel" on the CBC program. See note #2 above.

⁶ See note #2 above.

⁷ This remark comes from a discussion of her ideas before she reads from *CG, AC, PU* and *PP* on a 60 minute cassette tape made by High Barnett, Toronto, 1973. Atwood's concept of the self is described in Chapter I and discussed with reference to the fiction in Chapters V and VI.

⁸ Al Purdy, *The Cariboo Horses*, (Toronto: McClelland & Stewart Ltd., 1976), p. 11.

Chapter V

¹ "Interview with Margaret Atwood," Linda Sandler, *The Malahat Review*, 41 (January, 1977), p. 19. For a further discussion of her fiction see her interview with Graeme Gibson in *Eleven Canadian Novelists* (Toronto: Anansi, 1973).

² "Margaret Atwood: Poet as Novelist," *The Canadian Novel in the Twentieth Century* (Toronto: McClelland & Stewart Ltd., 1975), p. 314.

³ Margaret Atwood, *Dancing Girls* (Toronto: McClelland & Stewart Ltd., 1977). All further references are to this text. The

following eleven stories were previously published: "The War in the Bathroom," *Alphabet*, 8 (1964); "The Man from Mars," *Ontario Review* (Spring-Summer, 1977); "Polarities," *Tamarack Review*, 58 (1971), "Rape Fantasies," *The Fiddlehead*, 104 (Winter, 1975); "Under Glass," *Harper's*, 244 (February, 1972); "The Grave of the Famous Poet," *Oberon Press* (1972); "Hair Jewellry," *Ms. Magazine* (December, 1976); *Saturday Night*, 90 (May, 1975); "The Resplendent Quetzal," *The Malahat Review*, 41 (January, 1977); "Lives of the Poets," *Saturday Night* (April, 1977).

⁴ While I do not suggest that formal and thematic unity is the best, let alone only, way to prepare a collection of stories, it has proved remarkably effective in Alice Munro's *Lives of Girls and Women*, Margaret Laurence's *A Bird in the House*, Clark Blaise's *A North American Education* and Gabrielle Roy's *Rue Deschambault*.

⁵ Quoted from Atwood's introductory remarks on the cassette by High Barnett, Toronto, 1973.

⁶ Margaret Atwood, *The Edible Woman* (Toronto: McClelland & Stewart, 1969), p. 61. All quotations are taken from this edition and are included in the text.

⁷ Sandler, *The Malahat Review*, p. 24

⁸ Sandler, *The Malahat Review*, pp. 24-25

⁹ Sandler, *The Malahat Review*, p. 26

¹⁰ Sandler, *The Malahat Review*, pp. 13-14.

Chapter VI

¹ Gibson, pp. 20 and 22.

² *Surfacing* (New York: Simon and Schuster, 1972), p. 7. All further references are to this edition and are included in the text.

³ *The Malahat Review*, 41 (January, 1977), p. 12.

⁴ Gibson, p. 25

⁵ See, for example, Catharine McLay, "The Divided Self: Theme and Pattern in Margaret Atwood's *Surfacing*," *Journal of*

Canadian Fiction, IV, I (1975), pp. 82-95, and Carol P. Christ, "Margaret Atwood: The Surfacing of Women's Spiritual Quest and Vision," *Signs*, II, 2 (Winter, 1976), pp. 316-330.

⁶ From the High Barnett Tape, Toronto, 1973.

⁷ Gibson, p. 27.

⁸ Gibson, p. 29.

⁹ *Another Time* (Press Porcépic, 1977) p. 143. Mandel's essay, emphasizing duplicity and "reflexive pattern of story within story," is one of the most perceptive studies of Atwood to date.

Chapter VII

¹ "An Interview with Margaret Atwood," J. R. Struthers, *Essays on Canadian Writing*, 6 (Spring, 1977), p. 19 and p. 25.

² Atwood did not complete her thesis on Haggard, but in a lengthy article on his strange novel *She*, she emphasizes the 19th century tradition of tension between domestic and exotic in the male conception of woman that *She* dramatizes. Joan taps this tradition in her portraits of Charlotte and Felicia. "Superwoman Drawn and Quartered: The Early Forms of *She*," *Alphabet*, 10 (July 1965), pp. 65-82.

³ Struthers, *Essays on Canadian Writing*, p. 23.

⁴ Margaret Atwood explained something of the genesis of *Lady Oracle* to me during our discussion of her work in June, 1978.

⁵ *Lady Oracle* (Toronto: McClelland & Stewart, 1976), p.7. All references are to this edition.

⁶ Jane Austen, *Northanger Abbey* (Edinburgh: John Grant, 1911), p. 7.

⁷ Susan Howatch, *Call in the Night* (Connecticut: Fawcett, 1967), p. 168.

⁸ Iona and Peter Opie, *The Classic Fairy Tales* (London: Oxford University Press, 1974), p. 14.

⁹ There are several versions of the Bluebeard story. Atwood is

referring here to Grimm's "Fitcher's Bird" in which three sisters are stolen by a wizard. The first two enter the forbidden room, see the murdered wives, and are detected and butchered. The third sister outwits the wizard, brings her sisters to life, and escapes disguised as a bird. Perrault's "La Barbe Bleu," in *Perrault's Fairy Tales* (New York: Dover Publishing,Inc., 1969), also ends happily because the curious bride's brothers arrive just in time. For a brief discussion of the story and its historical analogues, see Opie, *The Classic Fairy Tales*.

[10] W. F. Jackson Knight, *Virgil: Epic and Anthropology* (London: George Allen and Unwin, 1967), p. 165. Atwood brought Knight's work to my attention in our talks of June, 1978.

[11] Knight, p. 253.

[12] Robert Graves, *The White Goddess: A Historical Grammar of Poetic Myth* (London: Faber and Faber, Ltd., 1948). Whether as the goddess of the three phases of the moon or as sky, earth and underworld, according to Graves, "the Triple Goddess ... was a personification of primitive woman — woman the creatress and destructress. As the New Moon or spring she was girl; as the Full Moon or summer she was woman; as the Old Moon or Winter she was hag" p. 384. In Bartok's opera, *The Castle of the Duke Bluebeard* (1911), the villain's wives are transformed into the three stages of the day—morning, noon, and evening, — while the fourth, Judith, becomes the night.

[13] Struthers, *Essays on Canadian Writing*, p. 21.

[14] Struthers, *Essays on Canadian Writing*, p. 25.

Chapter VIII

[1] Gibson, p. 12.

[2] In two discussions of Reaney, Atwood points out the importance of *Alphabet* as a typically Canadian product because of its synthesizing purpose, bringing together documentary and myth, as well as Reaney's Blakean ability to dramatize the relation of self to universe. See "Eleven Years of *Alphabet*", *Canadian Literature*, 49 (Summer, 1971), pp. 60-64, and "Reaney Collected" in *Poets and Critics*, ed. George Woodcock (Toronto: Oxford University Press,

1974), pp. 115-158.

³ I am very grateful to Margaret Atwood and Oxford University Press for allowing me to read the unedited typescript of this collection during the preparation of this chapter. Page references, however, are to the now published text: *Two-Headed Poems* (Toronto: Oxford University Press, 1978).

Postscript

¹ *Life Before Man* (Toronto: McClelland & Stewart, 1979). All references are included in the text.

² Lesje, however, has nothing of Mrs. Swithin's wisdom and faith, nor is she able to radiate the vision of harmony and goodness which makes Lucy Swithin a bulwark against the disillusionment or violence in life.

Selected Bibliography

Note: A complete Atwood bibliography is currently being prepared by Alan J. Horne for the *Annotated Bibliography of Canadian Literature*. His preliminary checklist appeared in *The Malahat Review*, 41 (January, 1977), pp. 195-222. I have listed below only Atwood's principal works plus those interviews and critical studies which I have found most useful. Complete references to all other works consulted appear in the Notes.

I.   PRIMARY

Atwood, Margaret. *The Animals in That Country*. Toronto: Oxford University Press, 1968.

————. *The Circle Game*. Toronto: Anansi, 1966; second edition, Anansi, 1978.

————. *Dancing Girls*. Toronto: McClelland & Stewart, 1977.

————. *Days of the Rebels: 1815-1840* in *Canada's Illustrated Heritage* series. Toronto: McClelland & Stewart, 1977.

————. *Double Persephone*. Toronto: Hawkshead Press, 1961.

————. *The Edible Woman*. Toronto: McClelland & Stewart, 1969.

————. *The Journals of Susanna Moodie*. Toronto: Oxford University Press, 1970.

————. *Lady Oracle*. Toronto: McClelland & Stewart, 1976.

————. *Life Before Man*. Toronto: McClelland & Stewart, 1979.

————. *Power Politics*. Toronto: Anansi, 1972.

————. *Procedures for Underground*. Toronto: Oxford University Press, 1970.

————. *Selected Poems*. Toronto: Oxford University Press, 1976.

————. *Surfacing*. New York: Simon and Schuster, 1972.

————. *Survival: A Thematic Guide to Canadian Literature*. Toronto: Anansi, 1972.

————. *Two-Headed Poems*. Toronto: Oxford University Press, 1978.

————. *Up in the Tree*. Toronto: McClelland & Stewart, 1978.

————. *You Are Happy*. Toronto: Oxford University Press, 1974.

II SECONDARY

Allen, Carolyn. "Margaret Atwood: Power of Transformation, Power of Knowledge," *Essays on Canadian Writing*, 6 (Spring, 1977), 5-17.

Campbell, Josie P. "The Woman as Hero in Margaret Atwood's *Surfacing*," *Mosaic*, XI, 3 (Spring, 1978), 17-28.

Christ, Carol P. "Margaret Atwood: The Surfacing of Women's Spiritual Quest and Vision," *Signs*, II, 2 (Winter, 1976), 316-330.

Cude, Wilf. "The Truth was not Convincing," *The Fiddlehead*, 112 (Winter, 1977), 133-137.

Davey, Frank. "Atwood's Gorgon Touch," *Studies in Canadian Literature*, II, 2 (Summer, 1977), 146-163.

Garebian, Keith. "*Surfacing*: Apocalyptic Ghost Story," *Mosaic*, 3 (Spring, 1976), 1-9.

Gerstenberger, Donna. "Conceptions Literary and Otherwise," *Novel*, 9 (Winter, 1976), 141-150.

Gibson, Graeme. *Eleven Canadian Novelists*. Toronto: Anansi, 1973, 1-31.

Kroetsch, Robert. "Unhiding the Hidden," *Journal of Canadian Fiction*, III, 3 (1974), 43-45.

Mandel, Eli. "Atwood Gothic," *Another Time*. Erin, Ontario: Press Porcépic Ltd., 137-145

McLay, Catherine. "The Divided Self: Theme and Pattern in Margaret Atwood's *Surfacing*," *Journal of Canadian Fiction*, IV, 1, 82-95.

Onley, Gloria. "Power Politics in Bluebeard's Castle," *Canadian Literature*, 60 (Spring, 1974), 21-42.

Purdy, Al. "Atwood's Moodie," *Canadian Literature*, 47 (Winter, 1971), 80-84.

Rogers, Linda. "Margaret the Magician," *Canadian Literature*, 60 (Spring, 1974), 83-86.

Rubenstein, Roberta. "Surfacing: Margaret Atwood's Journey to the Interior," *Modern Fiction Studies*, 22 (Autumn, 1976), 387-399.

Ross, Gary. "The Circle Game," *Canadian Literature*, 60 (Spring, 1974), 51-63.

Sandler, Linda. "Interview with Margaret Atwood," *The Malahat Review*, 41 (January, 1977), 7-27.

Schaeffer, Susan Fromberg. " 'It is Time That Separates Us': Margaret Atwood's *Surfacing*," *Centennial Review*, 18 (Fall, 1974), 319-337.

Scott, Andrew. "The Poet as Sorceress," *Essays on Canadian Writing*, 3 (Fall, 1975), 60-62.

Struthers, J. R. "An Interview with Margaret Atwood," *Essays on Canadian Writing*, 6 (Spring, 1977), 18-27.

Sullivan, Rosemary. "Breaking the Circle," *The Malahat Review*, 41 (January, 1977), 30-41.

Thomas, Clara. "Feminist or Heroine," *Essays on Canadian Writing*, 6 (Spring, 1977), 28-31.

van Varsveld, Gail. "Talking with Atwood," *Room of One's Own*, 1 (Summer, 1975), 66-70.

Wood, Susan. "The Martian Point of View," *Extrapolation*, 15 (May, 1974), 161-173.

Woodcock, George. "Poet as Novelist," *The Canadian Novel in the Twentieth Century*. Toronto: McClelland & Stewart, 1975, 312-327.

TAPES

Margaret Atwood. Atwood reads from *CG, AC, PU* and *PP* with useful introductory remarks. Cassette tape, 60 minutes. Toronto: High Barnett, 1973.

"The Twist of Feeling." Atwood discusses *PP*, with readings by Gwen Thomas, November, 1971.

Index

Note on the Author

Sherrill Grace lives in Vancouver and teaches Modern and Canadian literature at University of British Columbia. She has written articles on Canadian writers, including the Introduction to the Anansi reprint of *The Circle Game* (1978) by Margaret Atwood, and on Malcolm Lowry. She is currently co-editing a collection of critical essays on the work of Margaret Atwood.